Contents

Preface

The root of this book, as with so many things, started with a journey. I already knew in basic terms what I wanted to do: combine existing poetry with my own Celtic artwork. The idea had been swirling around for some time. Having built up a body of artwork over the last three and a half years, sufficient in number to form a strong basis for a book – and with enough ideas for further pieces – I knew that the only question for me now was in my choice of poems. As always, other work had to be completed first and my ideas were forced to wait before they could take shape. Then came the offer of joining a motorcycling tour of Ireland. Having just finished an illustration project that had been taking up to twelve hours a day, seven days a week, I jumped at the chance to get some fresh air and not look at a pencil or paintbrush for a while! After some 1,500 miles of travelling, amassing long-lasting memories along the way, and coming across people and places both old and new to me, I was finally sure of the form I wanted this book to take and what it should contain.

This led to my second and, in some respects, longer journey as I began to search for poems to use alongside my artwork. I had already picked up some ideas along the way in Ireland, both specific pieces as well as general works of a particular poet. Others came later, mainly from collections and anthologies spanning the last thousand years or more. I certainly cannot claim that the result is a scholarly collection reflecting literary merit or with a historical basis. It merely reflects my personal choices, often based upon little more than gut reaction to pieces I felt were suitable. In one case I mean this quite literally, as the poem's inclusion is inspired from the best restaurant meal I have ever had: its presence in the collection reminds me of that town, the bay and the sun setting over the mountains. I do not always like to do things conventionally and, having read more than a thousand poems to arrive at this final collection, my selection processes have been as eclectic as, hopefully, the resulting anthology is.

Before I began the research for this book, many of the pieces and poets were unknown to me. My literary journey contained the joy of discovery, of stepping into new territory, just as my physical journey through Ireland had (though thankfully without quite as many literary bumpy roads and potholes). It is hoped that those readers who also find here pieces new to them may be encouraged to hunt out further works by some of the authors, or to research the myths contained within the poems in more depth, so beginning their own individual journey of discovery.

Chris Down

Acknowledgements

I would like to thank the following for their permission to use copyright material: Thomas Kinsella for extracts from *The Táin*, his translations of poems by Aogán Ó Rathaille and Eoghan Rua Ó Súilleabháin, and for quoting parts of his translation guide from *the Táin*; Sheed & Ward Ltd for 'The Mason' from *The First Exile* by Robert Farren; David Higham Associates Ltd. for 'Cushenden', 'Prayer Before Birth', 'Tree Party' and 'Woods' by Louis MacNeice from *The Collected Poems of Louis MacNeice*, Faber & Faber Ltd.; 'Amairgin's Song of Ireland' reproduced by permission of Caitlín Matthews, from *The Encyclopeadia of Celtic Wisdom*, Element Books 1994; 'The Wooing of Etain', 'Pleasant the House', 'The Deserted Mountain' and 'Under Sorrows Sign' from *The Faber Book of Irish Verse* ed. John Montague reprinted by permission of The Peters Fraser and Dunlop Group Limited on behalf of John Montague; The Estate of Padraic Colum for 'Plougher'and 'She Moved Through the Fair' from *The Poet's Circuits*, Dolmen Press; Faber and Faber Ltd. for 'The Forge' from *Door into the Dark* by Seamus Heaney, Copyright © 1969 Seamus Heaney, 'The Pitchfork' from *Seeing Things* by Seamus Heaney, Copyright © 1991 Seamus Heaney, 'The Otter'and 'Sloe Gin' from *New Selected Poems 1966-1987* by Seamus Heaney, Copyright © 1990 Seamus Heaney (for the US 'The Pitchfork', 'The Otter' and 'Sloe Gin' by Seamus Heaney with the permission of Farrer, Straws & Giroux, inc.); 'Address to an old Wooden Gate', 'Living in the Country', 'To the Man After the Harrow', 'Peace' and 'Stony Grey Soil' by kind permission of the Trustees of the Estate of Patrick Kavanagh, c/o Peter Fallon, Literary Agent, Loughcrew, Oldcastle, Co. Meath, Ireland; 'Caoilte', 'The Hermit's Song', 'Kilcash', 'The Praise of Fionn' and 'Winter' from *The Penguin Book of Irish Verse* reprinted by permission of The Peters Fraser and Dunlop Group Limited on behalf of the Estate of Frank O'Connor; A.P. Watt on behalf of Michael Yeats for 'Fergus and the Druid', 'The Hosting of the Sidhe', 'The Lake Isle of Innisfree', 'The Secret Rose', 'The Song of Wandering Aengus', 'The Stolen Child' and 'The Wild Swans at Coole' from *The Collected Poems of W.B. Yeats*, Penguin Books. For the U.S. edition, the work of W.B. Yeats is reprinted with the permission of Scribner, a division of Simon & Schuster, from *The Collected works of W.B. Yeats, Vol. 1: The Poems*, revised by Richard J. Finneran (New York: Scribner 1997).

I would also like to thank Stuart Booth at Cassell for seeing the project through, John Matthews for recommending me to Stuart in the first place, Pete Douglas at Tantra Designs, my parents for support over the years above and beyond the call of duty and, finally, thanks to Paul and Yvette for the time in Ireland where this all began.

Introduction

We all have dreams, whether they are the unbidden, fantastical journeys of the night or the longing ambitions of the day. Although they are very different, each in its own way reflects the hopes and fears of the subconscious. While such dreams, especially the daytime wanderings, look to a future – or a possible future at least – their roots are planted firmly in the past. We are built upon the experiences of where we have been, and the footsteps of those who have walked the path before us. I once met someone who believed that the teaching of history at school was a waste of time, that even knowledge of history was pointless. This was in the late 1980s when it was thought that all that mattered was knowledge of numbers and commerce. He was wrong then and still is now. We ignore the past at our peril, as it is our guide to the future. We must learn from previous mistakes, continue to do those things we know are right, and try to understand why some events occurred as they did.

This particular book is firmly embedded in the past. Some of the poems and verse date back in their written form to the sixth century AD, and further back in their original, orally transmitted, guise. Whether the past presented here is real or imagined – sometimes it is, at best, a fanciful notion of what could have been, while at other times it is locked in hardbound reality – it is still a view of that past that is being given. Hence the sub-title *Visions of a Past*, not the past. Another person's compilation would have given a different vision – a no less valid one, as there can be no definitive viewpoint.

As for that particular past, the myths explored within the poems of the first section, 'The Mists of Time', though not based upon historical fact, reflect in part the culture which originally created those myths. We should not forget, however, that we are often seeing that culture through the eyes of the monastic translators and subsequent re-interpreters who have re-written again for their own contemporaries. This becomes more complicated when we realize that those contemporaries could well have been eighteenth-century readers, thus rendering the poems even more obscure to the modern mind.

The artwork too, although all created over the last three and a half years, is touched by influences stretching back over many centuries, to a time when the illuminated gospels were first being created, and beyond. The artwork styles and patterns contained within those ancient manuscripts did not appear overnight. They were themselves a progression of artforms that had gone before. In its early stages, Celtic art was more three-dimensional, and was more likely to take the form of metalwork, enamelling, and carvings. Its style and patterning was more akin to Art Nouveau than the now recognized animal and ribbon interlace, which is actually more Germanic than Celtic in origin. The whole progression from simple metal images to manuscript took over a thousand years. Just as the twentieth-century artist of the Celtic style looks to the older manuscripts for inspiration and details on which to base their contemporary designs, so the monastic artists and illustrators looked to earlier artwork styles. Whether Celtic art is a reworking – akin to a literary translation – or a new design, the result always reaches back to another age, and is just as much a product of then as well as the present.

When I first considered producing this book, I happily admit that it was as a vehicle for my artwork. For, at this moment in time, the creation of the interlacing knots, spirals and beasts that are recognized around the world as Celtic artwork, is my primary form of artistic expression. However, I knew that the artwork alone would not be sufficient. Despite having a strong belief in these images, and the power their patterns have on the mind's eye, it needed something more. To combine my artwork with poetry, also of utmost importance in the Celtic world, was the ideal solution. I decided to put the two elements together in a form similar to the ancient manuscripts, separating them into sections with main illuminated title-pages, fully decorated carpet pages and the poems themselves would be presented with complementary artwork. I wanted each page to be decorated and laid out in such a way that it could be taken out of context and considered worthy of attention in its own right – if this is not overstating the case. I am content for the result to be considered a coffee-table book, to be dipped into at any point. My next task was to find a defining point for the poems I wished to include, like the hook line in a song, to be the point it revolves around.

The Celts in their heyday were truly pan-European, sweeping across the Continent, assimilating and sacking in equal measure. Their real importance was ignored for a long time, and for centuries they were considered barbarians because of their lack of use of the written word – a mistake made more than once throughout history and not just in regard to the Celts. Even a fledgling Rome had reason to fear them as they spread out from Central Europe. These people of Iron Age Europe would not have called themselves Celts. Indeed, modern scholars and archaeologists are even less likely to use the term. They could not be identified purely by race or even by language, particularly during the earlier periods. Today, they are more defined by what is known about their way of life, their beliefs and attitudes, as well as the artifacts of everyday life, which are now regarded as their artform.

As mentioned earlier, the written word was not used by the early Celts, and their stories, myths and poetry were only transcribed much later by Christian hands. As such, the transcripts do not completely reflect the true nature of those orally transmitted words and a degree of interpretation is needed to find their true meaning, if that is possible. Consequently, the aspect of Celtic life which has best survived through the millennia is their art. Many items have been recovered, ranging from the hoards found at La Tène (Switzerland) and Hallstatt (Austria) – these have become defining points in Celtic categorization – to individual pieces, which can be seen in their full state (the ravages of time and the elements not withstanding) in museums or in the pages of books. As the Celts moved through Europe and the centuries passed, their art was adapted, assimilated and changed. It was a gradual process. The modern ethos of always being new, challenging and changing did not apply. As with most 'un-westernized' cultures, continuity and a sense of place was valued and any change developed over decades or centuries, not months. Furthermore, boundaries between arts and crafts disappeared. To the Celts their art was part of everyday life, and they decorated even the most simple objects. Art was not the preserve of an elite, where only those who can understand or afford it can appreciate it.

As the first millennium progressed the Celtic world declined, having been forced out or conquered in many places, but the art continued to develop and took on new influences, most notably the Germanic animal inter-lace and new expression in the form of the early Christian manuscripts. The arrival of Christianity in the British Isles prompted a virtual renaissance in Celtic art, providing new influences and reasons for creativity. A culture which had relied on oral tradition for the dissemination of knowledge, where the poet could have the status of a king and a warrior be shamed from the battle-field by satire, had finally met the written word. As a result, the ultimate form of Celtic artistic expression was born in the shape of the illuminated gospels.

It is at this point, in a way, that *Celtic Dreams* starts: when the first monks started to record some of the traditions and myths of the earlier Celts. It was a time when the last of the Celtic race had been pushed into the west-ern seaboard of the British Isles, Brittany and the island of Ireland. In Ireland the Celtic line to the past has remained the least broken: it may be battered but it is intact, despite nearly 800 years of occupation which, at times, sought to eradicate all that was Gaelic. Allied to that survival is a poetic tradition, which reaches from those early monks' transcripts, through the decline of bardic poetry in the seventeenth century, out into the world of Anglo-Irish domi-nance and arrives finally in the era of Yeats and beyond.

It was in Ireland that I found my defining point for this volume. I did not ignore the other Celtic homelands lightly, but the Irish line contained such a wealth of material for me to choose from. I decided to include poems from writers of Irish or Anglo-Irish descent, who still represent that least broken Gaelic Celtic line.

It is my belief that from its contracted base, the Celtic influence is spreading once again. Not with the kind of dominance that swept through pre-Christian Europe, but more subtly. It has gone beyond the simplicity of the Celtic revivals of the nineteenth and early twentieth centuries and has emerged once more, for some, into everyday life. However, Celtic art is still not 'high art' for the enjoyment of an elitist few. It once more adorns everyday items including jewellery, pottery, materials, even skin in the form of tattoos and, of course, books. It is inherent to the ephemeral nature of modern society, that the popularity of Celtic art today will be replaced by something else tomorrow. However, for many it is an artform that is back here to stay, and not something to be seen merely behind the glass of a museum case or in a history book, as has been the case for so long.

T.W. Rollestone argues in his book *Celtic Myth and Legend*, that the term Anglo-Saxon as applied to the occupants of parts of the British Isles is misleading, in that it diminishes the role that the Celtic element has played in British history and subsequent British influence in the world. He suggests the idea of an Anglo-Celtic population is more accurate. This would integrate elements of a Germanic and a Celtic line, the Germanic/Teutonic part giving an order and rigidity to society, and the Celtic part being responsible for creativity and individuality. This idea also reflects the fact that the Saxons did not completely wipe out the Celts in the areas they occupied. For instance, in the Sutton Hoo ship burial – the most important Saxon archeological find on British soil to date – items of Celtic origin, such as hanging bowls possibly from Ireland, were found. This could simply indicate healthy trading connections, as items were found from Byzantine and Rhineland areas among others. However, (as indicated in Ruth and Vincent Magaw's *Celtic Art*) some of the Saxon jewellery contains an enamelling technique called *millefiori* used by the Celts since Roman times but not seen in Germanic jewellery until then. This suggests a link between Germanic and Celtic craftsmen, whether working together or influencing one another, and indicates a possibility of the Anglo-Celtic theme. I like this argument, but it seems unlikely that the notion of Anglo-Celtic will take hold; afterall, Rollestone put forward his idea around a hundred years ago and it hardly caught on then. However, I would like to think of the Anglo-Celtic trait as being reality, and that it is because of this the Celtic influences are pushing out from the Celtic fringe once more.

Celtic Dreams is split into three sections and these reflect three different themes. There is naturally some overlap between the sections, and some poems clearly express more than one theme. Broadly speaking, the first section 'The Mists of Time' is largely concerned with mythology and some history. It starts with 'Amairgin's song of Ireland' and the 'Lay of Fintan', both of which concern the invasion myths – a means of explaining the beginning of Irish history through myth rather than historical fact. Fintan tells of the different races to invade, the final race being the Milesians (Gaelic Celts). The Milesians were vying with the Tuatha De Danaan or the 'People of the Goddess Danu' for control of the land. The De Danaans were the gods and goddesses, later known as the Sidhe (originally the name of their dwelling places) who inhabited the earthworks, barrows and antiquarian sites of ancient Ireland. It was a time when pre-history met history as the Celtic migrants to Ireland encountered the remnants of neolithic and megalithic civilizations. Stories arose, concerning the origins and naming of these places as well as the people who inhabited them. This was possibly as a means of understanding what had gone before, but also to make sense of what they found there. The Celts also had a habit of adapting to the traditions and religious practices of those who inhabited the areas into which they moved. It is no wonder, when one considers the impressive megalithic sites of Newgrange, Callanish, Stonehenge and Avebury, as well as their many lesser cousins across the British Isles, that these places had an influence on Celtic thought. These sites, even now, contain a sense of mystery and are held in awe throughout western Europe. So it was in Ireland that the home of the Tuatha De Danaan gave rise to many tales and myths.

As well as the invasion myths there were other cycles or sagas, many now lost, others written down, after several centuries of oral transmission. The greatest of these is *The Táin Bo Cuailnge* or the Cattle Raid of Cooley. This is part of the Ulster cycle whose main hero is Cúchulainn, the Hound of Ulster. The last five poems in 'The Mists of Time' are taken from Thomas Kinsella's translation of *The Táin*. Also included here is Samuel Ferguson's 'Derdre's Lament for the Sons of Usnach' which relates the same events found in 'Derdriu's Reply', but with different spellings of names. Indeed, this is a problem with different recountings and sources, and throughout this volume spellings have been kept as in the original texts, and not made uniform throughout. In the appendices I have included a section which, in very brief detail, describes the events concerned with – and sometimes leading up to – some of the mythological poems. This is for those who are not already familiar with the backgrounds to some of the Celtic myths and want a greater understanding of the events being described. I find that just to have the text presented with no explanation of characters and plot can, in some cases, detract from the full enjoyment of the piece. A more detailed description is well beyond the scope of this book and was never its intention. There are a great many books already on Celtic mythologies, giving ample coverage of this field, some of which are included in the Bibliography. There is also an appendix to aid with the pronunciation of some of the Irish words, so that the poems to be read in a more accurate way. For instance the word *Sidhe* is in fact pronounced 'shee'. This, again, is brief, but to insert phonetic explanations of words into the poems would be disruptive, and, undoubtedly, mistakes would occur if I attempted to do so (I am an illustrator not a linguist!) There are of course then the instances where the authors or translators have themselves used the anglicized forms, such as *Ulster* (originally *Ulaidh*). This area is, in fact, a bit of a minefield, but trod carefully the reader should get through unscathed, as I would like to think I have done.

Another major group of stories is the Fenian or Ossianic cycle concerning Fionn mac Cumhaill and his son Ossian. These were set around the third century AD and, whereas the Ulster cycle, set at the time of Christ, is largely concerned itself with the strivings of mortal men and women (however fantastical), the Ossianic cycle is concerned with a supernatural Otherworld and its inhabitants. This is seen in 'The Land Oversea', and in 'The Hosting of the Sidhe', where Ossian is lured by Niamh to the Land of Youth (the Tuatha De Danaan also make another appearance here). The end of this era – when Ossian returns after a period of 300 years in the Otherworld and recounts his previous life in 'The Praise of Fionn' – also marks the arrival of St Patrick, Christianity and the eventual change within Ireland.

Through the expanding structure of the monastic settlements, great institutions in their own right, Ireland became an important seat of learning for the next few centuries. Not only did priests set out from there to spread the word of God, but would-be scholars throughout Europe made for Ireland, such was its high standing. Despite the perils of the time, such as Viking raids, these monastic centres provided the environment for the creation of the illuminated gospels. Some of the centres abroad were set up by Irish priests, such as Iona in Scotland, created by St Columba. Subsequently, monks from Iona helped convert Northumbria to Celtic Christianity and further great monasteries were created including Lindisfarne, home of the gospels second only to the Book of Kells. It was a time when Christian Ireland came to terms with its pagan past and, however dismissive the monks and priests were of the legitimacy of the sagas, they were finally written down. At the end of the Book of Leinster version of *The Táin* the copier wrote (in Latin), not only that it is a 'fantasy' full of 'devellish lies' and 'poetical figments' but that it was for the 'enjoyment of idiots'. Hardly a wholehearted endorsement.

Actually very few, if any, of the characters and events in the cycles can be considered to be of actual people and occurrences, and their value is a different one to that of historical learning. There is of course the problem of various interpretations and rewritings up to and including this century, in which individual authors have put their own mark. This has clouded the original intent and meaning of the stories, in much the same way that the Arthurian saga has become distorted over the years. Despite this, what remains tells of a time when pursuits of the intellect were held in the same regard as the warriors great fighting feats, where honour was held in high esteem such that a bond given could only be broken at great cost, where love caused some to risk all and where immortals walked among men. They also talk of insane jealousy, betrayal, revenge and complete bloodbaths – all the aspects of a good story from a time and race long considered barbarian and its art degenerate. See Appendix B on page 135 for explanatory notes on some of the poems in this section

The section 'Sacred Spaces' is earthbound and it concerns the land, the people who lived on it, and the way they lived (and still do in some cases). It is about nature's beauty and harshness. The earliest writing here is again from sixth- to tenth-century monastic scribes. 'The Hermit's Song' casts a particularly idyllic picture of places, such as Glendaloch in the Wicklow mountains where St Kevin resided as a hermit, until word got out and a monastic city arose to accommodate the faithful flocking in. I doubt if he considered the present tourist centre as he laid his head on a stone pillow beside the isolated lake accessible only by boat.

There are deliberate contrasts in 'Sacred Spaces'. This is important, since it is all too easy to paint a rose-tinted picture of nature and forget what it can be like in its entirety, especially in an age when central heating, electric lighting and glass windows cushion the harsher effects of the elements. Poems such as 'Winter' have hence been included to counterpoint the more idealistic poems such as 'The Hermit's Song'. The inclusion here of some of the works of Patrick Kavanagh is part of this policy of contrast, as well as paying homage to his importance in twentieth-century Irish poetry. His was a different view of the land: born and brought up in County Monaghan at the beginning of the century, and a farmer before a poet, he did not have the same views of rural idyll as other Irish poets before him. Kavanagh was at odds with ethereal works such as those of Yeats, as well as the nationalist issues of the time. He did not have much time for them. In fact, I have some doubts if he would have taken great comfort in being included in a compilation entitled *Celtic Dreams,* but I will take that risk. His inclusion here just touches the edges of his work. For instance, my use here of just the opening paragraph of 'Living in the Country' is intended to be ironic, as the rest of the work presents a dark, harsh view of rural life. As with his major work 'The Great Hunger' (1942), its scale and nature is beyond the scope of this book, but both poems are worth investigating as their breaking of the rural myth flew in the face of policies of the time – surely not a bad thing to do.

Beyond the land are the people and their emotions, ambitions and longings. 'Of Love and Freedom' contains the two poems I feel most strongly about – as soon as I read them I decided to conclude with them. 'The Rebel' and 'Prayer Before Birth' contain universal themes which are relevant to all, irrespective of time and place. This has been one of my prime aims with *Celtic Dreams*, to take poems whose roots are from a specific place or situation yet can have a relevance elsewhere. If it were a volume that only appealed to those with an interest in Irish history and mythology it would be too narrow in its approach.

This section contains the most political, deep-felt poems of the collection. Even those that appear to be simple love poems may hide a more profound meaning. Of course, they could also be just love poems, as not every thing has to have hidden meanings. Indeed, in the world of poetry love is quite often the order of the day. However, for a period in Ireland's history more important issues were burning. Scratch the surface of some poems and the reader will often find that a woman may symbolize Ireland, any rogue male represents England, and the hope contained is generally of a return to an earlier order. In the seventeenth to nineteenth centuries, to write in such metaphorical terms was the only way of expressing certain hopes and dreams. The works of Ó Rathaille and Ó Súilleabháin here are *aisling*, or vision poems, a term originated by Ó Rathaille as a means of articulating his desire for a Jacobite return in Ireland. To encounter such subjects, even on such a perfunctory visit to Irish poetry through the centuries is unavoidable. To ignore them is inexcusable. I have looked across 1,500 years of writing, and 800 of those years contain an English presence, the repercussions of which are very real and still with us today.

What percolates through these writings is the need for individual freedom, to be able to determine one's destiny and to maintain a level of personal expression. This is a Celtic attribute that cuts through the centuries and one that is not bound by race or language. One of the great strengths – and at the same time, weaknesses – of the early Celtic tribes was a love of individuality of the person and of the tribal unit. Even in the face of the Roman Empire it was rare for the tribes to gather together under a single chieftain and fight back. It was simply not in their nature. On the occasions that they did the results were devastating. For example, when the Romans betrayed the Celts at the siege of Clusium in 391BC (at this time the Romans were supposed to be in allegiance with the Celts against the Etruscans in northern Italy), the Celtic tribes marched, ignoring all other cities on the way, until they reached Rome. Once there, they sacked the city and occupied it for a year until suitable tribute and apologies were received. This kind of event was the exception rather than the norm, however. Although there was a sense of common identity amongst the Celtic peoples, no one from the tribe next door was going to determine what you did. It was very rare for an overall chieftain of the different tribal units to appear. Could this be one of the reasons that there has been a resurgence of interest in things Celtic in the late twentieth century? At a time, when large-scale corporations stretch across national boundaries, even continents, and have more power than many governments, is a sense of individuality and of self-determination manifesting itself again? Within some of these companies and institutions, both large and small, managers may determine how their employees appear, dress and behave – even out of the work environment in some cases – in order to hammer home a corporate identity. This appears to be becoming more prevalent – everything for the good of the company rather than the individual. Then there are those who feel otherwise.

It is interesting to watch Celtic and Roman battle re-enactment groups together and notice how polarized they are. The Roman legionnaires seem faceless in their identical uniforms, regimented to the highest degree as they march across the field of battle, near unstoppable in their ruthless efficiency. Then there are the Celts, proud individuals in dress and manner, men and women together as equals even on a battlefield, waving weapons and shouting indiscriminately. There is no doubt as to who is the most likely victor in such a confrontation. It is of course the Romans. Their empire stretched across much of Europe, North Africa and the Middle East at its peak. This does not mean that the Roman way is the right one simply because of its ability to turn soldiers into automatons, like marching ants. Even today, some groups, such as environmentalists and eco-warriors, like to think of themselves as free-willed as the Celts, fighting against the doctrinal establishments of government bodies and large-scale companies. An image I have seen used in various campaigns is of the cartoon character Asterix the Gaul tapping his head and saying 'these Romans are crazy'. The Roman Empire may now be dust, but 2,000 years later the spirit of the Celts lives on. Not in every way of course, since who wants a return to cattle raiding, head hunting and slavery to name but a few things best consigned to the history books?

And so there are those who aspire to what may be termed as a 'Celtic' way of life, even if they do not think of it as such themselves. After all, in many ways, the name is but a tag – just a process of categorizing people, artifacts and artwork. It does not matter if the general use of the term Celtic dies out – in much the same way that historians have become more reluctant to use it in reference to a historical people and their remains. It is much better to take something on its own individual merit. What is more important, is that the Celtic ethos survives: a love and respect for the land and environment and all that it contains; a sense of history and place; a wonder of what has gone before and the unknown; a state of independence and individuality, but also a sense of belonging within the tribal group (today known as a circle of friends) and not lost within a faceless rule-bound society. That is the dream.

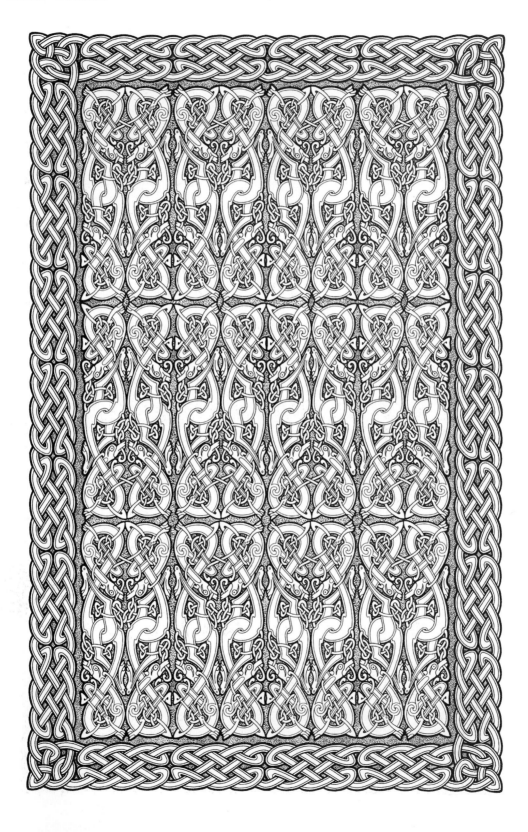

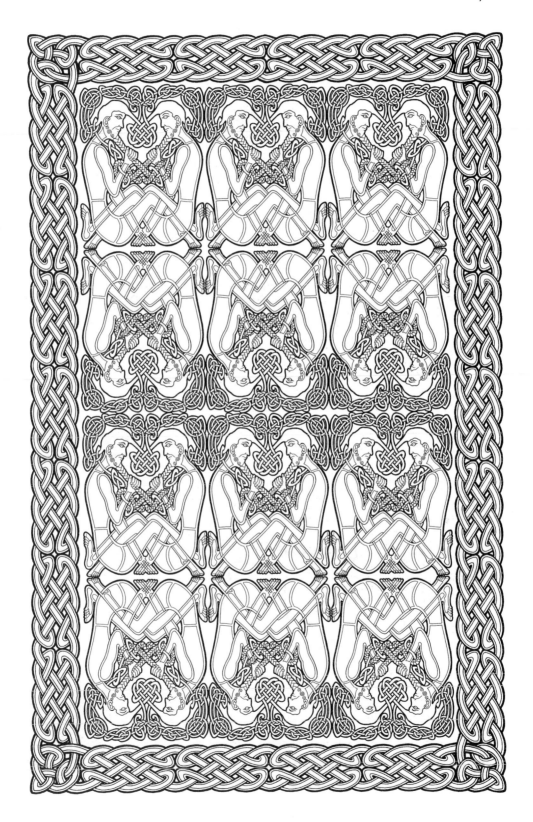

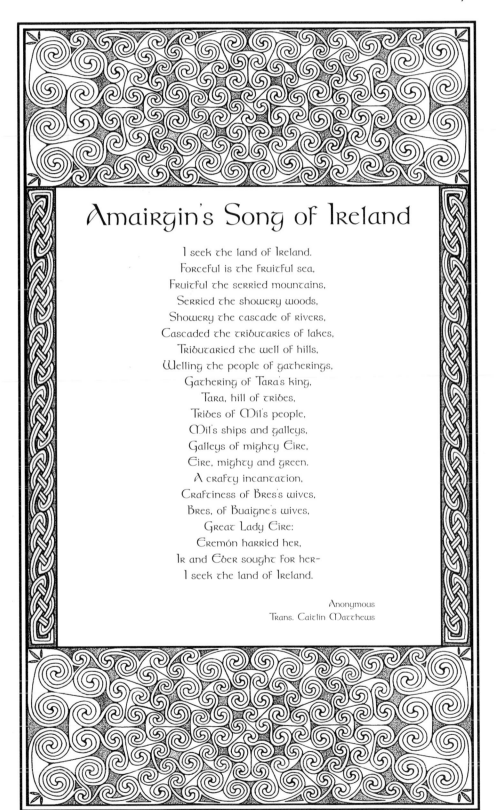

Amairgin's Song of Ireland

I seek the land of Ireland.
Forceful is the fruitful sea,
Fruitful the serried mountains,
Serried the showery woods,
Showery the cascade of rivers,
Cascaded the tributaries of lakes,
Tributaried the well of hills,
Welling the people of gatherings,
Gathering of Tara's king,
Tara, hill of tribes,
Tribes of Mil's people,
Mil's ships and galleys,
Galleys of mighty Eire,
Eire, mighty and green.
A crafty incantation,
Craftiness of Bres's wives,
Bres, of Buaigne's wives,
Great Lady Eire:
Eremón harried her,
Ir and Eber sought for her—
I seek the land of Ireland.

Anonymous
Trans. Caitlin Matthews

Lay of Fintan

Ireland, though it is enquired of me,
I know accurately
Every colonisation it has undergone
Since the beginning of the pleasant world.

Cessair came from the east,
The woman, daughter of Bith,
With her fifty maidens
And her trio of men.

The Deluge overtook them,
Though it was a sad pity,
And drowned them all
Each one on his height.

Bith north in Sliab Betha,
Sad was the mystery,
Ladru in Ard Ladrann,
Cessair in her recess.

As for me I was saved
By the Son of God, a protection over the throng,
The Deluge parted from me
Above massive Tul Tuinde.

I was a year under the Deluge
At bracing Tul Tuinde.
There has not been slept, there will not be,
Any better sleep.

Then Parthalon came to me
From the east, from the Grecian land,
And I lived on with his progeny
Though it was a long way.

I was still in Ireland
When Ireland was a wilderness,
Until Agnoman's son came,
Nemed, pleasant his ways.

Next came the Fir Bolg,
That is a fair true tale.
I lived together with them,
Whilst they were in the land.

The Fir Bolg and Fir Galion
Came, it was long [thereafter].
The Fir Domnann came,
They settled in Irrus in the west.

Then came the Tuatha Dé
In clouds of dark mist,
And I lived along with them
Though it was a long life.

The sons of Mil came then
Into the land against them
I was along with every tribe
Until the time ye see.

After that came the sons of Mil
Out of Spain from the south,
And I lived along with them
Though mighty was their combat.

I had attained to long life,
I will not hide it,
When the Faith came to me
From the King of the cloudy heaven.

I am white Fintan,
Bóchra's son, I will not hide it.
Since the Deluge here
I am a high noble sage.

Anonymous

The Hosting of the Sidhe

The host is riding from Knocknarea
And over the grave of Clooth-na-Bare;
Caoilte tossing his burning hair,
And Niamh calling Away, come away:
Empty your heart of its mortal dream.
The winds awaken, the leaves whirl round,
Our cheeks are pale, our hair is unbound,
Our breasts are heaving, our eyes are agleam,
Our arms are waving, our lips are apart;
And if any gaze on our rushing band,
We come between him and the deed of his hand,
We come between him and the hope of his heart.
The host is rushing 'twixt night and day,
And where is there hope or deed as fair?
Caoilte tossing his burning hair,
And Niamh calling Away, come away.

W.B. Yeats

The Land Oversea

Delightful is the land beyond all dreams,
Fairer than aught thine eyes have ever seen.
There all the year the fruit is on the tree,
And all the year the bloom is on the flower.

There with wild honey drip the forest trees;
The stores of wine and mead shall never fail.
Nor pain nor sickness knows the dweller there,
Death and decay come near him never more.

The feast shall cloy not, nor the chase shall tire,
Nor music cease for ever through the hall;
The gold and jewels of the Land of Youth
Outshine all splendours ever dreamed by man.

Thou shalt have horses of the fairy breed,
Thou shalt have hounds that can outrun the wind;
A hundred chiefs shall follow thee in war,
A hundred maidens sing thee to thy sleep.

A crown of sovranty thy brow shall wear,
And by thy side a magic blade shall hang,
And thou shalt be lord of all the Land of Youth,
And lord of Niam of the Head of Gold.

Anonymous

 # The Praise of Fionn

Patrick you chatter too loud
    And lift your crozier too high,
Your stick would be kindling soon
    If my son Osgar stood by.

If my son Osgar and God
    Wrestled it out on the hill
And I saw Osgar go down
    I'd say that your God fought well.

But how could the God you praise
    And his mild priests singing a tune
Be better than Fionn the swordsman,
    Generous, faultless Fionn?

Just by the strength of their hands
    The Fenians' battles were fought,
With never a spoken lie,
    Never a lie in thought.

There never sat priest in church
    A tuneful psalm to raise
Better spoken than these
    Scarred in a thousand frays.

Whatever your monks have called
    The law of the King of Grace,
That was the Fenians' law;
    His home is their dwelling-place.

If happier house than Heaven
    There be, above or below,
'Tis there my master Fionn
    And his fighting men will go.

Ah, priest, if you saw the Fenians
   Filling the strand beneath
Or gathered in steamy Naas
   You would praise them with every breath.

Patrick, ask of your God
   Does he remember their might,
Or has he seen east or west
   Better men in a fight?

Or known in his own land
   Above the stars and the moon
For wisdom, courage and strength
   A man the like of Fionn?

           Anonymous
      Trans. Frank O'Connor

Caoilte

Winter time is bleak, the wind
   Drives the stag from height to height;
Belling at the mountain's cold
   Untameable he strays tonight.

The old stag of Carren scarce
   Dare sleep within his den,
While the stag of Aughty hears
   Wolves call in every glen.

Long ago Osgar and I
   And Diarmuid heard that cry;
And we listened to the wolves
   As the frosty night went by.

Now the stag that's filled with sleep
   Lays his lordly side to rest
As if the earth had drawn him down
   To the winter's icy breast.

Though I drowse above the fire
   Many a winter morning drear
My hand was tight about a sword
   A battleaxe or spear.

And though I sleep cold tonight,
   God, I offer thanks to you
And to Christ, the Virgin's Son,
   For the mighty men I slew.

Anonymous
Trans. Frank O'Connor

The Stolen Child

Where dips the rocky highland
Of Sleuth Wood in the lake,
There lies a leafy island
Where flapping herons wake
The drowsy water-rats;
There we've hid our faery vats,
Full of berries
And of reddest stolen cherries.
Come away, O human child!
To the waters and the wild
With a faery, hand in hand,
For the world's more full of weeping
than you can understand.

Where the wave of moonlight glosses
The dim grey sands with light,
Far off by furthest Rosses
We foot it all the night,
Weaving olden dances,
Mingling hands and mingling glances
Till the moon has taken flight;
To and fro we leap
And chase the frothy bubbles,
While the world is full of troubles
And is anxious in its sleep.
Come away, O human child!
To the waters and the wild
With a faery, hand in hand,
For the world's more full of weeping
than you can understand.

Where the wandering water gushes
From the hills above Glen-Car,
In pools among the rushes
That scarce could bathe a star,
We seek for slumbering trout
And whispering in their ears
Give them unquiet dreams;
Leaning softly out
From ferns that drop their tears
Over the young streams.
Come away, O human child!
To the waters and the wild
With a faery, hand in hand,
For the world's more full of weeping
than you can understand.

Away with us he's going,
The solemn-eyed:
He'll hear no more the lowing
Of the calves on the warm hillside
Or the kettle on the hob
Sing peace into his breast,
Or see the brown mice bob
Round and round the oatmeal-chest.
For he comes, the human child!
To the waters and the wild
With a faery, hand in hand,
From a world more full of weeping
than he can understand.

W.B. Yeats

The Celts

Long, long ago, beyond the misty space
    Of twice a thousand years,
In Erin old there dwelt a mighty race,
    Taller than Roman spears;
Like oaks and towers they had a giant grace,
    Were fleet as deers,
With wind and waves they made their biding place,
    These western shepherd seers.

Their Ocean-God was Manannan MacLir,
    Whose angry lips,
In their white foam, full often would inter
    Whole fleets of ships;
Cromah their Day-God, and their Thunderer
    Made morning and eclipse;
Bride was their Queen of Song, and unto her
    They prayed with fire-touched lips.

Great were their deeds, their passions and their sports;
    With clay and stone
They piled on strath and shore those mystic forts,
    Not yet o'erthrown;
On cairn-crowned hills they held their council-courts;
    While youths alone,
With giant dogs, explored the elk resorts,
    And brought them down.

Of these was Fin, the father of the Bard
    Whose ancient song
Over the clamour of all change is heard,
    Sweet-voiced and strong.
Fin once o'ertook Grania, the golden-haired,
    The fleet and young;
From her the lovely, and from him the feared,
    The primal poet sprung.

Ossian! two thousand years of mist and change
  Surround thy name-
Thy Finian heroes now no longer range
  The hills of fame.
The very names of Fin and Gaul sound strange-
  Yet shine the same-
By miscalled lake and desecrated grange-
  Remains, and shall remain!

The Druid's alter and the Druid's creed
  We scarce can trace,
There is not left an undisputed deed
  of all your race,
Save your majestic song, which hath their speed,
  And strength and grace;
In that sole song, they live and love, and bleed-
  It bears them on through space.

O, inspired giant! shall we e'er behold,
  In our own time,
One fit to speak your spirit on the wold,
  Or seize your rhyme?
One pupil of the past, as mighty-souled
  As in the prime,
Were the fond, fair, and beautiful, and bold-
  They, of your song sublime!

Thomas D'Arcy McGee

A Vision of Connaught in the Thirteenth Century

I walked entranced
   Through a land of Morn;
The sun, with wondrous excess of light,
   Shone down and glanced
      Over seas of corn
And lustrous gardens aleft and right
   Even in the clime
      Of resplendent Spain,
Beams no such sun upon such a land;
   But it was the time,
      'Twas in the reign,
Of Cáhal Mór of the Wine-red Hand.

Anon stood high
   By my side a man
Of princely aspect and port sublime.
   Him queried I-
      'O, my lord and Khan,
What clime is this, and what golden time?
   When he - 'The clime
      Is a clime to praise,
The clime is Erin's, the green and bland;
   And it is the time,
      These be the days,
Of Cáhal Mór of the Wine-red Hand!

Then I saw thrones,
   And circling fires,
And a Dome rose near me, as by a spell,
   Whence flowed the tones
      Of silver lyres,
And many voices in wreathed swell;
   And their thrilling chime
      Fell on mine ears
As the heavenly hymn of an angel-band-
   It is now the time,
      These be the years,
Of Cáhal Mór of the Wine-red Hand!

I sought the hall,
    And, behold! – a change
From light to darkness, from joy to woe!
  King, nobles, all,
    Looked aghast and strange;
The minstrel-group sate in dumbest show!
  Had some great crime
    Wrought this dread amaze,
This terror? None seemed to understand
  'Twas then the time
    We were in the days,
Of Cáhal Mór of the Wine-red Hand.

I again walked forth,
    But lo! the sky
Showed fleckt with blood, and an alien sun
  Glared from the north,
    And there stood on high,
Amid his shorn beams, a skeleton!
  It was by the stream
    Of castled Maine,
One Autumn eve, in the Teuton's land,
  That I dreamed this dream
    Of the time and reign
Of Cáhal Mór of the Wine-red Hand!

                    James Clarence Mangan

The Sack of Baltimore

AD 1631

The summer sun is falling soft on Carbery's hundred isles—
The summer sun is gleaming still through Gabriel's rough defiles—
Old Inisherkin's crumbled fane looks like a moulting bird;
And in a calm and sleepy swell the ocean tide is heard;
The hookers lie upon the beach; the children cease their play;
The gossips leave the little inn; the households kneel to pray—
And full of love, and peace, and rest – its daily labour over—
Upon that cosy creek there lay the town of Baltimore.

A deeper rest, a starry trance, has come with midnight there;
No sound, except that throbbing wave, in earth, or sea, or air.
The massive capes, and ruined towers, seemed conscious of the calm;
The fibrous sod and stunted trees are breathing heavy balm.
So still the night, these two long barques, round Dunashad that glide,
Must trust their oars – methinks not few – against the ebbing tide—
Oh some sweet mission of true love should urge them to the shore—
They bring some lover to his bride, who sighs in Baltimore!

All, all asleep within each roof along that rocky street,
And these must be the lover's friends with gentle gliding feet—
A stifled gasp! a dreamy noise! 'the roof is in a flame!'
From out their beds, and to their doors, rush maid, and sire, and dame—
And meet, upon the threshold stone, the gleaming sabres' fall,
And over each black and bearded face the white or crimson shawl—
The yell of 'Allah' breaks above the prayer, and shriek and roar—
Oh, blessed God! the Algerine is lord of Baltimore!

Then flung the youth his naked hand against the shearing sword;
Then sprung the mother on the brand with which her son was gored;
Then sunk the grandsire on the floor, his grandbabes clutching wild;
Then fled the maiden moaning faint and nestled with the child:
But see, yon pirate strangled lies, and crushed with splashing heel,
While over him, in an Irish hand, there sweeps his Syrian steel,
Though virtue sink, and courage fail, and misers yield their store,
There's one hearth well avengèd in the sack of Baltimore!

Midsummer morn, in woodland nigh, the birds begin to sing—
They see not now the milking maids — deserted is the spring!
Midsummer day — this gallant rides from distant Bandon's town—
These hookers crossed from stormy Schull, that skiff from Affadown;
They only found the smoking walls, with neighbours' blood besprint,
And on the strewed and trampled beach awhile they wildly went—
Then dashed to sea, and passed Cape Clere, and saw five leagues before
The pirate galleys vanishing, that ravaged Baltimore.

Oh! some must tug the galleys over, and some must tend the steed—
This boy will bear a Sheik's chibouk, and that a Bey's jerreed.
Oh! some are for the arsenals, by beauteous Dardenelles;
And some are in the caravan to Mecca's sandy dells.
The maid that Bandon gallant sought is chosen for the Dey
She's safe — he's dead — she stabbed him in the midst of his serai;
And, when to die a death of fire that noble maid they bore,
She only smiled — O'Driscoll's child — she thought of Baltimore.

'Tis two long years since sunk the town beneath that bloody band,
And now amid its trampled hearths a larger concourse stand,
Where, high upon a gallows tree, a yelling wretch is seen—
'Tis Hackett of Dungarvan — he who steered the Algerine!
He fell amid a sullen shout, with scarce a passing prayer,
For he had slain the kith and kin of many a hundred there—
Some muttered of MacMurchaidh, who brought the Norman over—
Some cursed him with Iscariot, that day in Baltimore.

Thomas Davis

The Wife of Llew

And Gwydion said to Math, when it was Spring:
'Come now and let us make a wife for Llew.'
And so they broke broad boughs yet moist with dew,
And in a shadow made a magic ring:
They took the violet and the meadowsweet
To form her pretty face, and for her feet
They built a mound of daisies on a wing,
And for her voice they made a linnet sing
In the wide poppy blowing for her mouth.
And over all they chanted twenty hours.
And Llew came singing from the azure south
And bore away his wife of birds and flowers.

Francis Ledwidge

Pleasant the House

Pleasant the house where
men, women, and children
are swayed by the fair
and yellow haired Creide;

with a swift moving groom,
a door-keeper and butler to
carve when the druid sits
among the musicians . . .

Berries drip into the bowl
to dye her black shawl.
She has a crystal vat,
pale goblets and glasses.

Lime white, her skin;
quilts line her rushy floor,
silk, her blue cloak,
red gold, her drinking horn.

Her sun room glitters with
yellow gold and silver,
under warm ridged thatch
tufted brown and scarlet.

Two door posts of green
you pass, a shapely hinge,
and the beam of her lintel
far famed for its silver.

More lovely still, her chair,
On the left as you enter,
with a filigree of Alpine gold
round the foot of her bed.

To the right, another bed,
wrought from precious metals,
a hyacinthine canopy,
bronze curtain rods . .

A hundred foot from front
to back is the span
of the house of Creide;
twenty, her noble doorway.

Anonymous
Version John Montague

The Wooing of Etain

Fair lady, will you travel
To the marvellous land of stars?
Pale as snow the body there,
Under a primrose crown of hair.

No one speaks of property
In that glittering community:
White teeth shining, eyebrows black,
The foxglove hue on every cheek.

The landscape bright and speckled
As a wild bird's eggs–
However fair Ireland's Plain,
It is sad after the Great Plain!

Warm, sweet streams water the earth,
And after the choicest of wine and mead,
Those fine and flawless people
Without sin, without guilt, couple.

We can see everyone
Without being seen ourselves:
It is the cloud of Adam's transgression
Conceals us from mortal reckoning.

O woman if you join my strong clan,
Your head will hold a golden crown.
Fresh killed pork, new milk and beer,
We shall share, O Lady Fair!

Anonymous
Version John Montague

The Song
of Wandering Aengus

I went out to the hazel wood,
Because a fire was in my head,
And cut and peeled a hazel wand,
And hooked a berry to a thread;
And when white moths were on the wing,
And moth-like stars were flickering out,
I dropped the berry in a stream
And caught a little silver trout.

When I had laid it on the floor
I went to blow the fire aflame,
But something rustled on the floor,
And some one called me by my name:
It had become a glimmering girl
With apple blossom in her hair
Who called me by my name and ran
And faded through the brightening air.

Though I am old with wandering
Through hollow lands and hilly lands,
I will find out where she has gone,
And kiss her lips and take her hands;
And walk among long dappled grass,
And pluck till time and times are done
The silver apples of the moon,
The golden apples of the sun.

W.B. Yeats

Fergus and the Druid

Fergus. This whole day have I followed in the rocks,
And you have changed and flowed from shape to shape,
First as a raven on whose ancient wings
Scarcely a feather lingered, then you seemed
A weasel moving on from stone to stone,
And now at last you wear a human shape,
A thin grey man half lost in gathering night.

Druid. What would you, king of the proud Red Branch kings?

Fergus. This would I say, most wise of living souls:
Young subtle Conchubar sat close by me
When I gave judgement, and his words were wise,
And what to me was burden without end,
To him seemed easy, so I laid the crown
Upon his head to cast away my sorrow.

Druid. What would you, king of the proud Red Branch kings?

Fergus. A king and proud! and that is my despair.
I feast amid my people on the hill,
And pace the woods, and drive my chariot-wheels
In the white border of the murmuring sea;
And still I feel the crown upon my head.

Druid. What would you, Fergus?

Fergus. Be no more a king
But learn the dreaming wisdom that is yours.

Druid. Look on my thin grey hair and hollow cheeks
And on these hands that may not lift the sword,
This body trembling like a wind-blown reed.
No woman's loved me, no man's sought my help.

Fergus. A king is but a foolish labourer
Who wastes his blood to be another's dream.

Druid. Take, if you must, this little bag of dreams;
Unloose the cord, and they will wrap you round.

Fergus. I see my life go drifting like a river
From change to change; I have been many things—
A green drop in the surge, a gleam of light
Upon a sword, a fir-tree on a hill,
An old slave grinding at a heavy quern,
A king sitting upon a chair of gold—
And all these things were wonderful and great;
But now I have grown nothing, knowing all.
Ah, Druid, Druid, how great webs of sorrow
Lay hidden in the small slate-coloured thing!

W.B. Yeats

Deirdre's Lament
for the Sons of Usnach

The lions of the hill are gone,
And I am left alone – alone –
Dig the grave both wide and deep,
For I am sick, and fain would sleep!

The falcons of the wood are flown,
And I am left alone – alone –
Dig the grave both deep and wide,
And let us slumber side by side.

The dragons of the rock are sleeping,
Sleep that wakes not for our weeping:
Dig the grave and make it ready;
Lay me on my true Love's body.

Lay their spears and bucklers bright
By the warriors' sides aright;
Many a day the Three before me
On their linkèd bucklers bore me.

Lay upon the low grave floor,
'Neath each head, the blue claymore;
Many a time the noble Three
Reddened those blue blades for me.

Lay the collars, as is meet,
Of their greyhounds at their feet;
Many a time for me have they
Brought the tall red deer to bay.

Oh! to hear my true Love singing,
Sweet as sound of trumpets ringing:
Like the sway of ocean swelling
Rolled his deep voice round our dwelling.

Oh! to hear the echoes pealing
Round our green and fairy sheeling,
When the Three, with soaring chorus,
Passed the silent skylark o'er us.

Echo now, sleep, morn and even-
Lark alone enchant the heaven!-
Ardan's lips are scant of breath,-
Neesa's tongue is cold in death.

Stag, exult on glen and mountain-
Salmon, leap from loch to fountain-
Heron, in the free air warm ye-
Usnach's Sons no more will harm ye!

Erin's stay no more you are,
Rulers of the ridge of war;
Never more 'twill be your fate
To keep the beam of battle straight.

Woe is me! by fraud and wrong-
Traitors false and tyrants strong-
Fell Clan Usnach, bought and sold,
For Barach's feast and Conor's gold!

Woe to Eman, roof and wall!-
Woe to Red Branch, hearth and hall!-
Tenfold woe and black dishonour
To the false and foul Clan Conor!

Dig the grave both wide and deep,
Sick I am, and fain would sleep!
Dig the grave and make it ready,
Lay me on my true Love's body.

Samuel Ferguson

Derdriu's Reply

Conchobor, what are you thinking, you
That piled up sorrow over woe?
Truly, however long I live,
I cannot spare you much love.

The thing most dear to me in the world,
The very thing I most loved,
Your harsh crime took from me.
I will not see him till I die.

I feel his lack, wearily,
The son of Uisliu. All I see—
Black boulders on fair flesh
So bright once among the others.

Red-cheeked, sweet as the river-brink;
Red-lipped; brows beetle-black;
Pearly teeth gleaming bright
With a noble snowy light.

His figure easiest to find
Bright among Alba's fighting-men
- A border made of red gold
Matched his handsome crimson cloak.

A soft multitude of jewels
In the satin tunic - itself a jewel:
For decoration, all told,
Fifty ounces of light gold.

He carried a gold-hilted sword
And two javelins sharply tipped,
A shield rimmed with yellow gold
With a knob of silver at the middle.

Fergus did an injury
Bringing us over the great sea.
How his deeds of valour shrank
When he sold honour for a drink!

If all Ulster's warriors
Were gathered on this plain, Conchobor,
I would gladly give them all
For Noisiu, son of Uisliu.

Break my heart no more today.
In a short while I'll be no more.
Grief is heavier than the sea,
If you were but wise Conchobor.

From *The Táin*
Trans. Thomas Kinsella

Fedelm's Prophesy

I see a battle: a blond man
With much blood about his belt.
And a hero-halo round his head.
His brow is full of victories.

Seven hard heroic jewels
Are set in the iris of his eye.
His jaws are settled in a snarl.
He wears a looped, red tunic.

A noble countenance I see,
Working effect on womenfolk;
A young man of sweet colouring;
A form dragonish in the fray.

His great valour brings to mind
Cúchulainn of Murtheimne,
The hound of Culann, full of fame.
Who he is I cannot tell
But I see, now, the whole host
Coloured crimson by his hand.

A giant on the plain I see,
Doing battle with the host,
Holding in each of his two hands
Four short quick swords.

I see him hurling against that host
Two gea bolga and a spear
And an ivory-hilted sword,
Each weapon to its separate task.

He towers on the battlefield
In breastplate and red cloak.
Across the sinister chariot-wheel
The Warped Man deals death—
That fair form I first beheld
Melted to a mis-shape.

I see him moving to the fray:
Take warning, watch him well,
Cúchulainn, Sualdam's son!
Now I see him in pursuit.

Whole hosts he will destroy,
Making dense massacre.
In thousands you will yield your heads.
I am Fedelm. I hide nothing.
The blood starts from warrior's wounds
- Total ruin - at his touch:
Your warriors dead, the warriors
Of Deda mac Sin prowling loose;
Torn corpses, women wailing,
Because of him - the Forge-Hound.

From *The Táin*
Trans. Thomas Kinsella

The Morrigan

Dark one are you restless
    Do you guess they gather
To certain slaughter
    The wise raven
Groans aloud
    That enemies infest
The fair fields
    Ravaging in packs
Learn I discern
    Rich plains
Softly wavelike
    Bearing their necks
Greenness of grass
    Beauty of blossoms
On the plains of war
    Grinding heroic
Hosts to dust
    Cattle groans the Badb
The raven ravenous
    Among corpses of men
Affliction and outcry
    And war everlasting
Raging over Cuailnge
    Death of sons
Death of kinsmen
    Death death!

From *The Táin*
Trans. Thomas Kinsella

The Charioteer's Chant

I hear a chariot creaking.
I see its yoke of silver
And the great trunk of a man
    Above the hard prow.
The shafts jut forward,
They are approaching us
By the place of the tree-stump,
    Triumphant and proud.

There's a skilled Hound at the helm,
A fine chariot-warrior,
A wild hawk hurrying
    his horses southward.
Surely it is Cúchulainn's
Chariot-horses coming.
Who says he is not
    coming to our defeat?

I had a dream last year:
Whoever, at the time appointed,
Opposes the Hound on the slope,
    Let him beware.
The Hound of Emain Macha,
In all his different shapes,
The Hound of plunder and battle
    – I hear him, and he hears.

FROM *The Táin*
Trans. Thomas Kinsella

Cúchulainn's Lament

Ferdia, dead by their deceit,
Our last meeting I lament.
You are dead and I must live
To mourn my everlasting loss.

When we were away with Scáthach
Learning victory overseas,
It seemed our friendship would remain
Unbroken till the day of doom.

I loved the noble way you blushed,
And I loved your fine, perfect form.
I loved your blue clear eye,
Your way of speech, your skillfulness.

Your like, crimson son of Daman,
Never moved to the tearing fray,
Never was seized with manly wrath
Nor bore shield on his broad back.

Never till this very day,
Ferdia, did I ever find
Your match for great deeds in battle
Since I slew Aife's only son.

Medv's daughter Finnabair,
Whatever beauty she may have,
She was an empty offering,
A string to hold the sand, Ferdia.

Ferdia of the hosts and the hard blows,
Beloved golden brooch,
I mourn your conquering arm
And our fostering together.

You were a sight
To please a prince;
Your gold-rimmed shield,
Your slender sword,

The ring of bright silver
On your fine hand,
Your skill at chess,
Your flushed, sweet cheek,

Your curled yellow hair
Like a lovely jewel,
The leaf-shaped belt
You wore at your waist.

You fell to the Hound,
And I mourn, little calf.
The shield didn't save you
That you brought to the fray.

Shameful our struggle,
The grief and uproar!
O fair, fine hero
Who shattered armies
And crushed them under foot,
Golden brooch, I mourn.

From *The Táin*
Trans. Thomas Kinsella

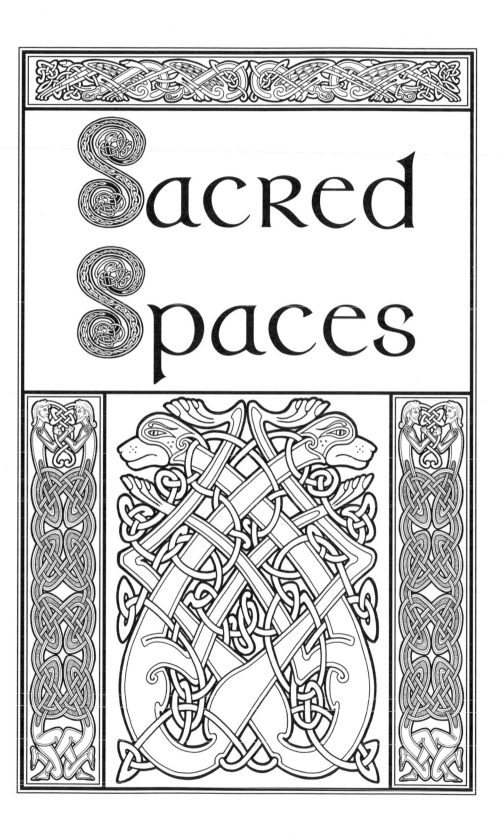

Sacred Spaces

The Meeting of the Waters

There is not in the wide world a valley so sweet
As that vale in whose bosom the bright waters meet;
Oh! the last rays of feeling and life must depart,
Ere the bloom of that valley shall fade from my heart.

Yet it was not that Nature had shed o'er the scene
Her purest of crystal and brightest of green;
'Twas not her soft magic of streamlet or hill,
Oh! no, -it was something more exquisite still.

'Twas that friends, the belov'd of my bosom, were near,
Who made every dear scene of enchantment more dear,
And who felt how the best charms of nature improve,
When we see them reflected from looks that we love.

Sweet vale of Avoca! how calm could I rest
In thy bosom of shade, with the friends I love best,
Where the storms that we feel in this cold world should cease,
And our hearts, like thy waters, be mingled in peace.

Thomas Moore

The Hermit's Song

A hiding tuft, a green-barked yew-tree
   Is my roof,
While nearby a great oak keeps me
   Tempest-proof.

I can pick my fruit from an apple
   Like an inn,
Or can fill my fist where hazels
   Shut me in.

A clear well beside me offers
   Best of drink,
And there grows a bed of cresses
   Near its drink.

Pigs and goats, the friendliest neighbours,
   Nestle near,
Wild swine come, or broods of badgers,
   Grazing deer.

All the gentry of the country
   Come to call!
And the foxes come behind them,
   Best of all.

To what meals the woods invite me
   All about!
There are water, herbs and cresses,
   Salmon, trout.

A clutch of eggs, sweet mast and honey
   Are my meat,
Heathberries and whortleberries
   For a sweet.

All that one could ask for comfort
   Round me grows,
There are hips and haws and strawberries,
   Nuts and sloes.

And when summer spreads its mantle
    What a sight!
Marjoram and leeks and pignuts,
    Juicy, bright.

Dainty redbreasts briskly forage
    Every bush,
Round and round my hut there flutter
    Swallow, thrush.

Bees and beetles, music-makers,
    Croon and strum;
Geese pass over, duck in autumn,
    Dark streams hum.

Angry wren, officious linnet
    And black-cap,
All industrious, and the woodpecker's
    Sturdy tap.

From the sea the gulls and herons
    Flutter in,
While in upland heather rises
    The grey hen.

In the year's most brilliant weather
    Heifers low
Through green fields, not driven nor beaten,
    Tranquil, slow.

In wreathed boughs the wind is whispering,
    Skies are blue,
Swans call, river water falling
    Is calling too.

               Anonymous
          Trans. Frank O'Connor

The Lake Isle of Innisfree

I will arise and go now, and go to Innisfree,
And a small cabin build there, of clay and wattles made:
Nine bean-rows will I have there, a hive for the honey-bee,
And live alone in the bee-loud glade.

And I shall have some peace there, for peace comes dropping slow,
Dropping from the veils of the morning to where the cricket sings;
There midnight's all a glimmer, and noon a purple glow,
And evening full of the linnet's wings.

I will arise and go now, for always night and day
I hear lake water lapping with low sounds by the shore;
While I stand on the roadway, or on the pavements grey,
I hear it in the deep heart's core.

W.B. Yeats

The Wild Swans at Coole

The trees are in their autumn beauty,
The woodland paths are dry,
Under the October twighlight the water
Mirrors a still sky;
Upon the brimming water among the stones
Are nine-and-fifty swans.

The nineteenth autumn has come upon me
Since I first made my count;
I saw, before I had well finished,
All suddenly mount
And scatter wheeling in great broken rings
Upon their clamorous wings.

I have looked upon those brilliant creatures,
And now my heart is sore.
All's changed since I, hearing at twilight,
The first time on this shore,
The bell-beat of their wings above my head,
Trod with a lighter tread.

Unwearied still, lover by lover,
They paddle in the cold
Companionable streams or climb the air;
Their hearts have not grown old;
Passion or conquest, wander where they will
Attend upon them still.

But now they drift on the still water,
Mysterious, beautiful;
Among what rushes will they build,
By what lake's edge or pool
Delight men's eyes when I awake some day
To find they have flown away?

W.B. Yeats

Winter

Winter is a dreary season,
Heavy waters in confusion
Beat the wide world's strand.
Birds of every place are mournful
But the hot and savage ravens,
At rough winter's shriek.
Crude and black and dank and smoky;
Dogs about their bones are snarling,
On the fire the cauldron bubbles
All the long dark day.

Anonymous
Trans. Frank O'Connor

Storm at Sea

Tempest on the plain of Lir
Bursts its barriers far and near,
 And upon the rising tide
 Wind and noisy winter ride-
Winter throws a shining spear.

When the wind blows from the east
All the billows seem possessed,
 To the west they storm away
 To the farthest, wildest bay
Where the light turns to its rest.

When the wind is from the north
The fierce and shadowy waves go forth,
 Leaping, snarling at the sky,
 To the southern world they fly
And the confines of the earth.

When the wind is from the west
All the waves that cannot rest
 To the east must thunder on
 Where the bright tree of the sun
Is rooted in the ocean's breast.

When the wind is from the south
The waves turn to a devil's broth,
    Crash in foam on Skiddy's beach,
    For Caladnet's summit reach,
Batter Limerick's grey-green mouth.

Ocean's full! The sea's in flood,
Beautiful is the ship's abode;
    In the Bay of the Two Beasts
    The sandy wind in eddies twists,
The rudder holds a shifting road.

Every bay in Ireland booms
When the flood against it comes-
    Winter throws a spear of fire!
    Round Scotland's shores and by Cantyre
A mountainous surging chaos glooms.

God's Son of hosts that none can tell
The fury of the storm repel!
    Dread Lord of the sacrament,
    Save me from the wind's intent,
Spare me from the blast of Hell.

Anonymous
Trans. Frank O'Connor

Kilcash

What shall we do for timber?
　　The last of the woods is down.
Kilcash and the house of its glory
　　And the bell of the house are gone,
The spot where that lady waited
　　Who shamed all women for grace
When earls came sailing to greet her
　　And Mass was said in the place.

My grief and my affliction
　　Your gates are taken away,
Your avenue needs attention,
　　Goats in the garden stray.
The courtyard's filled with water
　　And the great earls where are they?
The earls, the lady, the people
　　Beaten into the clay.

No sound of duck or geese there,
　　Hawk's cry or eagle's call,
No humming of the bees there
　　That brought honey and wax for all,
Nor even the song of the birds there
　　When the sun goes down in the west,
No cuckoo on top of the boughs there,
　　Singing the world to rest.

There's mist there tumbling from branches,
    Unstirred by night and by day,
And darkness falling from heaven,
    For our fortune has ebbed away,
There's no holly nor hazel nor ash there,
    The pasture's rock and stone,
The crown of the forest has withered,
    And the last of its game is gone.

I beseech of Mary and Jesus
    That the great come home again
With long dances danced in the garden,
    Fiddle music and mirth amongst men,
That Kilcash the home of our fathers
    Be lifted on high again,
And from that to the deluge of waters
    In bounty and peace remain.

Anonymous
Trans. Frank O Connor

Address to an Old Wooden Gate

Battered by time and weather; scarcely fit
For firewood; there's not a single bit
Of paint to hide those wrinkles, and such scringes
Break hoarsely on the silence - rusty hinges:
A barbed wire clasp around one withered arm
Replaces the old latch, with evil charm.
That poplar tree you hang upon is rotten,
And all its early loveliness forgotten.
This gap ere long must find another sentry
If the cows are not to roam the open country.
They'll laugh at you, Old Wooden Gate, they'll push
Your limbs asunder, soon, into the slush.
Then I will lean upon your top no more
To muse, and dream of pebbles on a shore,
Or watch the fairy-columned turf-smoke rise
From white-washed cottage chimneys heaven-wise.
Here have I kept fair tryst, and kept it true,
When we were lovers all, and you were new;
And many a time I've seen the laughing-eyed
Schoolchildren, on your trusty back astride.
But Time's long silver hand has touched our brows,
And I'm the scorned of women - you of cows.
How can I love the iron gates which guard
The fields of wealthy farmers? They are hard,
Unlovely things, a-swing on concrete piers-
Their finger-tips are pointed like old spears.
But you and I are kindred, Ruined Gate,
For both of us have met the self-same fate.

Patrick Kavanagh

June

Broom out the floor now, lay the fender by,
And plant this bee-sucked bough of woodbine there,
And let the window down. The butterfly
Floats in upon the sunbeam, and the fair
Tanned face of June, the nomad gypsy, laughs
Above her widespread wares, the while she tells
The farmers' fortunes in the fields, and quaffs
The water from the spider-peopled wells.

The hedges are all drowned in green grass seas,
And bobbing poppies flare like Elmo's light,
While siren-like the pollen-stainéd bees
Drone in the clover depths. And up the height
The cuckoo's voice is hoarse and broke with joy.
And on the lowland crops the crows make raid,
Nor fear the clappers of the farmer's boy,
Who sleeps, like drunken Noah, in the shade.

And loop this red rose in that hazel ring
That snares your little ear, for June is short
And we must joy in it and dance and sing,
And from her bounty draw her rosy worth.
Ay! soon the swallows will be flying south,
The wind wheel north to gather in the snow,
Even the roses spilt on youth's red mouth
Will soon blow down the road all roses go.

Francis Ledwidge

Plougher

Sunset and silence! A man; around him earth savage, earth broken;
Beside him two horses, a plough!

Earth savage, earth broken, the brutes, the dawn-man there in the sunset,
And the plough that is twin to the sword, that is founder of cities!

Brute-tamer, plough-maker, earth-breaker! Canst hear? There are ages between us—
Is it praying you are as you stand there alone in the sunset?

Surely our sky-born gods can be nought to you, earth-child and earth-master—
Surely your thoughts are of Pan, or of Wotan, or Dana?

Yet why give thought to the gods? Has Pan led your brutes where they stumble?
Has Dana numbed pain of the child-bed, or Wotan put hands to your plough?

What matter your foolish reply? O man standing lone and bowed earthward,
Your task is a day near its close. Give thanks to the night-giving god.

Slowly the darkness falls, the broken lands blend with the savage;
The brute-tamer stands by the brutes, a head's breadth only above them.

A head's breadth? Aye, but therein is hell's depth and the height up to heaven,
And the thrones of the gods and their halls, their chariots, purples, and splendours.

Padraic Colum

To the Man After the Harrow

Now leave the check-reins slack,
The seed is flying far today-
The seed like stars against the black
Eternity of April clay.

This seed is potent as the seed
Of knowledge in the Hebrew Book,
So drive your horses in the creed
Of God the Father as a stook.

Forget the men on Brady's hill.
Forget what Brady's boy may say
For destiny will not fulfil
Unless you let the harrow play.

Forget the worm's opinion too
Of hooves and pointed harrow-pins,
For you are driving your horses through
The mist where Genesis begins.

Patrick Kavanagh

Stony Grey Soil

O stony grey soil of Monaghan
The laugh from my love you thieved;
You took the gay child of my passion
And gave me your clod-conceived.

You clogged the feet of my boyhood
And I believed that my stumble
Had the poise and stride of Apollo
And his voice my thick-tongued mumble.

You told me the plough was immortal!
O green-life-conquering plough!
Your mandril strained, your coulter blunted
In the smooth lea-field of my brow.

You sang on steaming dunghills
A song of cowards' brood,
You perfumed my clothes with weasel itch,
You fed me on swinish food.

You flung a ditch on my vision
Of beauty, love and truth.
O stony grey soil of Monaghan
You burgled my bank of youth!

Lost the long hours of pleasure
All the women that love young men.
O can I still stroke the monster's back
Or write with unpoisoned pen

His name in these lonely verses
Or mention the dark fields where
The first gay flight of my lyric
Got caught in a peasant's prayer.

Mullahinsha, Drummeril, Black Shanco—
Wherever I turn I see
In the stony grey soil of Monaghan
Dead loves that were born for me.

Patrick Kavanagh

Living in the Country

Opening

It was the Warm Summer, that landmark
In a child's mind, an infinite day
Sunlight and burnt grass
Green grasshoppers on the railway slopes
The humming of wild bees
The whole summer during the school holidays
Till the blackberries appeared.
Yes, a tremendous time that summer stands
Beyond the grey finities of normal weather.

Patrick Kavanagh

Woods

My Father who found the English landscape tame
Had hardly in his life walked in a wood,
Too old when first he met one; Malory's knights,
Keat's nymphs or the Midsummer Night's Dream
Could never arras the room, where he spelled out True and Good
With their interleaving of half-truths and not-quites.

While for me from the age of ten the socketed wooden gate
Into a Dorset planting, into a dark
But gentle ambush, was an alluring eye;
Within was a kingdom free from time and sky,
Caterpillar webs on the forehead, danger under the feet,
And the mind adrift in a floating and rustling ark

Packed with birds and ghosts, two of every race,
Trills of love from the picture-book - Oh might I never land
But here, grown six foot tall, find me also a love
Also out of the picture-book; whose hand
Would be soft as the webs of the wood and on her face
The wood-pigeon's voice would shaft a chrism from above.

So in a grassy ride a rain-filled hoof-mark coined
By a finger of sun from the mint of Long Ago
Was the last of Lancelot's glitter. Make-believe dies hard;
That the rider passed here lately and is a man we know
Is still untrue, the gate to Legend remains unbarred,
The grown-up hates to divorce what the child joined.

Thus from a city when my father would frame
Escape, he thought, as I do, of bog or rock
But I have also this other, this English, choice
Into what yet is foreign; whatever its name
Each wood is the mystery and the recurring shock
Of its dark coolness is a foreign voice.

Yet in using the word tame my father was maybe right,
These woods are not the Forest; each is moored
To a village somewhere near. If not of today
They are not like the wilds of Mayo, they are assured
Of their place by men; reprieved from the neolithic night
By gamekeepers or by Herrick's girls at play.

And always we walk out again. The patch
Of sky at the end of the path grows and discloses
An ordered open air long ruled by dyke and fence,
With geese whose form and gait proclaim their consequence,
Pargetted outposts, windows browed with thatch,
And cow pats - and inconsequent wild roses.

Louis MacNeice

Tree Party

Your health, Master Willow. Contrive me a bat
To strike a red ball; apart from that
In the last resort I must hang my harp on you.

Your health, Master Oak. You emblem of strength,
Why must your doings be done at such length?
Beware lest the ironclad ages catch up with you.

Your health, Master Blackthorn. Be live and be quick.
Provide the black priest with a big black stick
That his ignorant flock may go straight for the fear of you.

Your health, Master Palm. If you brew us some toddy
To deliver us out of by means of the body,
We will burn all our bridges and rickshaws in praise of you.

Your health, Master Pine. Though sailing be past
Let you fly your own colours upon your own mast
And rig us a crow's nest to keep a look out from you.

Your health, Master Elm. Of giants arboreal
Poets have found you the most immemorial
And yet the big winds may discover the fault in you.

Your health, Master Hazel. On Hallow-e'en
Your nuts are to gather but not to be seen
Are the twittering ghosts that perforce are alive in you.

Your health, Master Holly. Of all the trees
That decorate parlour walls you please
Yet who would have thought you had so much blood in you?

Your health, Master Apple. Your topmost bough
Entices us to come climbing now
For all that old rumour there might be a snake in you.

Your health, Master Redwood. The record is yours
For the girth that astounds, the sap that endures,
But where are the creatures that once came to nest in you?

Your health, Master Banyn, but do not get drunk
Or you may not distinguish your limbs from your trunk
And the sense of Above and Below will be lost on you

Your health, Master Bo-Tree. If Buddha should come
Yet again, yet again make your branches keep mum
That his words yet again may drop honey by leave of you.

Your health, Master Yew. My bones are few
And I fully admit my rent is due,
But do not be vexed, I will postdate a cheque for you.

Louis MacNeice

The Mason

Nothing older than stone but the soil and the sea and the sky.
Nothing stronger than stone but water and air and fire.
Nothing worthier than stone but the harpstring, the word and the tree.
Nothing humbler or stubborner than stone- whatever it be!

Stone is the bone of the world, under moor, under loam,
Under ocean and churchyard-corruption of buried bone;
Floor of the mountain, pound of the ocean, the world's cord.
God's creature, stone, that once was the vault of its Lord.
God gave me stone to know for a womb with child,
The time of delivery come but waiting the knife:
I free the stone-borne glory into the air,
Rounded and grooved and edged and grained and rare.

I have mastered the grain, the make, the temper of stone,
Fingering it and considering, touching with hand and with soul,
Quarrying it out of the course, piercing and severing it,
With a chirp of meeting metals like a bird's chirp.

Basalt I know - bottle-green still pools of stone
Harder than hawk's beak, shark's tooth or tusk of the boar;
Basalt - the glass-stone, stone without pore or wart;
Causeway-stone stepped across Moyle-fjord in the north.

Granite I know - dust-pearl with silver eyes-
That moulds domed hills, with snow, rain, wind and time.
Marble - the multiple-tinted, - the satin-flesh-
Daughter of the King of white Greece in the lands of the west.

Dark flint I know with the feel of a fox's tongue,
The unconsumed cold carrier of fire its young,
Stone of hairedges and thornpoints, the dagger stone,
Spearstone, swordstone, hatchet-stone, hearth-gilly stone.

O Christ, the stone which the builders rejected
And which is become the head of the corner,
Part me from them the stone shall grind when it fall;
Leave me not a stone in thine enemies' hand!

Robert Farren

The Forge

All I know is a door into the dark.
Outside, old axles and iron hoops rusting;
Inside, the hammered anvil's short-pitched ring,
The unpredictable fantail of sparks
Or hiss when a new shoe toughens in water.
The anvil must be somewhere in the centre,
Horned as a unicorn, at one end square,
Set there immovable: an altar
Where he expends himself in shape and music.
Sometimes, leather-aproned, hairs in his nose,
He leans out on the jamb, recalls a clatter
Of hoofs where traffic is flashing in rows;
Then grunts and goes in, with a slam and flick
To beat real iron out, to work the bellows.

Seamus Heaney

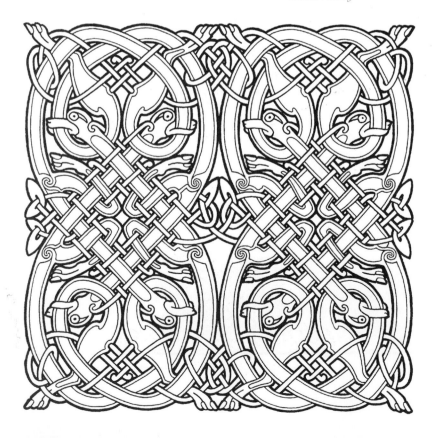

The Pitchfork

Of all implements, the pitchfork was the one
That came near to an imagined perfection:
When he tightened his raised hand and aimed with it,
It felt like a javelin, accurate and light.

So whether he played the warrior or the athlete
Or worked in earnest in the chaff and sweat,
He loved its grain of tapering, dark-flecked ash
Grown satiny from its own natural polish.

Riveted steel, turned timber, burnish, grain,
Smoothness, straightness, roundness, length and sheen.
Sweat-cured, sharpened, balanced, tested, fitted.
The springiness, the clip and dart of it.

And then when he thought of probes that reached the farthest,
He would see the shaft of a pitchfork sailing past
Evenly, imperturbably through space,
Its prongs starlit and absolutely soundless—

But has learned at last to follow that simple lead
Past its own aim, out to an other side
Where perfection - or nearness to it - is imagined
Not in the aiming but the opening hand.

Seamus Heaney

The Otter

When you plunged
The light of Tuscany wavered
And swung through the pool
From top to bottom.

I loved your wet head and smashing crawl,
Your fine swimmer's back and shoulders
Surfacing and surfacing again
This year and every year since.

I sat dry-throated on the warm stones.
You were beyond me.
The mellowed clarities, the grape-deep air
Thinned and disappointed.

Thank God for the slow loadening,
When I hold you now
We are close and deep
As the atmosphere on water.

My two hands are plumbed water.
You are my palpable, lithe
Otter of memory
In the pool of the moment.

Turning to swim on your back,
Each silent, thigh-shaking kick
Re-tilting the light,
Heaving the cool at your neck.

And suddenly you're out,
Back again, intent as ever,
Heavy and frisky in your freshened pelt,
Printing the stones.

Seamus Heaney

Sloe Gin

The clear weather of juniper
darkened into winter.
She fed gin to sloes
and sealed the glass container.

When I unscrewed it
I smelled the disturbed
tart stillness of a bush
rising through the pantry.

When I poured it
it had a cutting edge
and flamed
like Betelgeuse.

I drink to you
in smoke-mirled, blue-black,
polished sloes, bitter
and dependable.

Seamus Heaney

Magdalen Walks

The little white clouds are racing over the sky,
    And the fields are strewn with the gold of the flower of March,
    The daffodil breaks under foot, and the tasselled larch
Sways and swings as the thrush goes hurrying by.

A delicate odour is borne on the wings of the morning breeze,
    The odour of deep wet grass, and of brown new-furrowed earth,
    The birds are singing for joy of the Spring's glad birth,
Hopping from branch to branch on the rocking trees.

And all the woods are alive with the murmur and sound of Spring,
    And the rose-bud breaks into pink on the climbing briar,
    And the crocus-bed is a quivering moon of fire
Girdled round with the belt of an amethyst ring.

And the plane to the pine-tree is whispering some tale of love
    Till it rustles with laughter and tosses its mantle of green,
    And the gloom of the wych-elm's hollow is lit with the iris sheen
Of the burnished rainbow throat and the silver breast of a dove.

See! the lark starts up from his bed in the meadow there,
    Breaking the gossamer threads and the nets of dew,
    And flashing a-down the river, a flame of blue!
The kingfisher flies like an arrow, and wounds the air.

Oscar Wilde

The Deserted Mountain

A gloomy thought, Ben Bulben,
shapely crested mountain;
before old Tall Crook came
how lovely shone your peak.

Many hounds and gillies
strayed on your slopes;
many strong warriors heard
the hoarse hunting horn.

The pack's cry in the glens
on the wild boar's track:
every Fenian was followed
by lovely, leashed hounds.

Many a sweet-strung harp
was struck on your green sward,
the well made tale or poem
with gold was always matched.

The heron's lament by night,
the moorhen in the heather—
how sweet it was to hear
their melodies twine together.

It would lift your heart
to hear the eagle's cry,
the sweet chant of the otters,
the yelp of jack foxes.

At that time, Ben Bulben,
no one shunned your lofty sides.
Tonight, I have few companions,
of my kindred none survives.

Your blackbirds and thrushes,
an amulet against loneliness:
dove clusters in your branches
comforted sorrowing women.

Many's the time these same
fair Fenian women gathered
fragrant tasting blackberries
from your tangled brambles.

Bogberries, brightly scarlet,
brookline, cuckoo spit and cress:
the daughters of the King of Ulster
hummed sweetly at their harvest.

Honeysuckle and black sloes,
hazel, pignut and woodbine;
those were marching rations
when the Fianna roamed Erin.

Lovely inlets of water,
sweet free running streams;
though tonight a spent veteran,
I lived in pleasant times.

Anonymous
Trans. John Montague

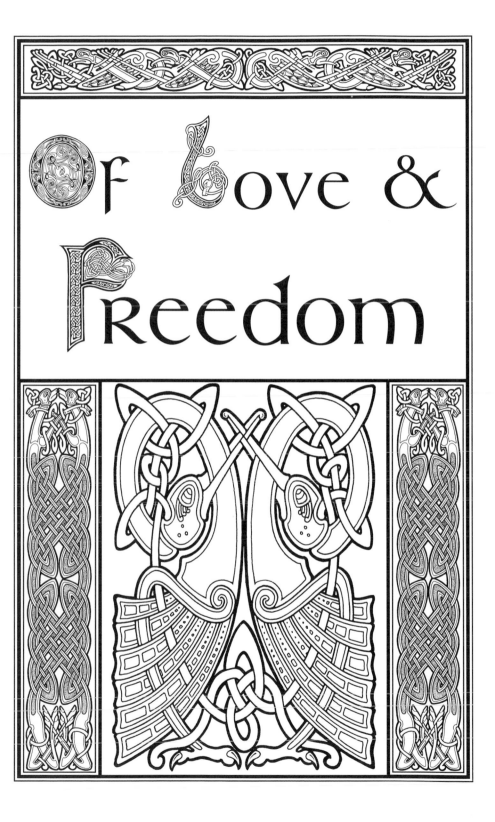

Of Love & Freedom

The Secret Rose

Far-off, most secret, and inviolate Rose,
Enfold me in my hour of hours; where those
Who sought thee in the Holy Sepulchre,
Or in the wine-vat, dwell beyond the stir
And tumult of defeated dreams; and deep
Among pale eyelids, heavy with the sleep
Men have named beauty. Thy great leaves enfold
The ancient beards, the helms of ruby and gold
Of the crowned Magi; and the king whose eyes
Saw the Pierced Hands and Rood of elder rise
In Druid vapour and make the torches dim;
Till vain frenzy awoke and he died; and him
Who met Fand walking among flaming dew
By a grey shore where the wind never blew,
And lost the world and Emer for a kiss;
And him who drove the gods out of their liss,
And till a hundred morns had flowered red
Feasted, and wept the barrows of his dead;
And the proud dreaming king who flung the crown
And sorrow away, and calling bard and clown
Dwelt among wine-stained wanderers in deep woods;
And him who sold tillage, and house, and goods,
And sought through lands and islands numberless years,
Until he found, with laughter and with tears,
A woman of so shining loveliness
That men threshed corn at midnight by a tress,
A little stolen tress. I, too, await
The hour of thy great wind of love and hate.
When shall the stars be blown about the sky,
Like the sparks blown out of the smithy, and die?
Surely thine hour has come, thy great wind blows,
Far-off, most secret, and inviolate Rose?

W.B. Yeats

Ireland

I called you by sweet names by wood and linn,
You answered not because my voice was new,
And you were listening for the hounds of Finn
    And the long hosts of Lugh.

And so, I came unto a windy height
And cried my sorrow, but you heard no wind,
For you were listening to small ships in flight,
    And the wail on hills behind.

And then I left you, wandering the war
Armed with will, from distant goal to goal,
To find you at the last free as of yore,
    Or die to save your soul.

And then you called to us from far and near
To bring your crown from out the deeps of time,
It is my grief your voice I couldn't hear
    In such a distant clime.

Francis Ledwidge

 # Peace

And sometimes I am sorry when the grass
Is growing over the stones in quiet hollows
And the cocksfoot leans across the rutted cart-pass
That I am not the voice of country fellows
Who now are standing by some headland talking
Of turnips and potatoes or young corn
Or turf banks stripped for victory.
Here Peace is still hawking
His coloured combs and scarves and beads of horn.

Upon a headland by a whinny hedge
A hare sits looking down a leaf-lapped furrow
There's an old plough upside-down on a weedy ridge
And someone is shouldering home a saddle-harrow.
Out of that childhood country what fools climb
To fight with tyrants Love and Life and Time?

Patrick Kavanagh

Cushendun

Fuchsia and ragweed and the distant hills
Made as it were out of clouds and sea:
All night the bay is splashing and the moon
    Marks the break of the waves.

Limestone and basalt and a whitewashed house
With passages of great stone flags
And a walled garden with plums on the wall
    And a bird piping in the night.

Forgetfulness: brass lamps and copper jugs
And home-made bread and the smell of turf or flax
And the air a glove and the water lathering easy
    And convulvulus in the hedge.

Only in the dark green room beside the fire
With the curtains drawn against the winds and waves
There is a little box with a well-bred voice:
    What a place to talk of War.

Louis MacNeice

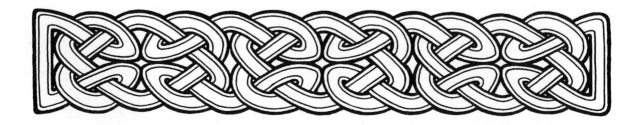

Under Sorrow's Sign

A pregnant girl, under sorrow's sign,
Condemned to a cell of pain,
Bore, by leave of Creation's Lord,
Her small child in prison.

Swiftly the young lad flourished,
Eager as a bardic novice,
For those first years in prison,
Clear as if we were looking on.

Who would not be moved, alas,
As he darts playful little runs
Within the limit of his walls
While his mother falls into sadness!

For all daylight brought to them—
O sharp plight – was the glimpse
A single augurhole might yield
Of the bright backbone of a field.

Seeing one day on her pale face
A shining tear, the child cried:
'Unfold to me your sorrow
Since I follow its trace.

Does there exist another world
Brighter than where we are:
A home lovelier than this
Source of your heavy weariness?'

'Seeing the narrow track we tread
Between the living and the dead
It would be small wonder if I
Were not sad, heedless boy.

But had you shared my life
Before joining this dark tribe
Then on the tender hobbyhorse
Of your soul, sorrow would ride.

The flame of the wide world
Warmed my days at first;
To be closed in a dark cell
Afterwards: that's the curse.'

Realising this life's distress
Beyond all balm or sweetness,
The boy's brow did not darken
Before his cold and lonely prison.

This image – this poem's dungeon:
Of those closed in a stern prison
These two stand for the host of living
Their sentence, life imprisonment.

Against the gaiety of God's son,
Whose kingdom holds eternal sway
Sad every dungeon where earth's hosts
Lie hidden from the light of day.

Gofraidh Fionn O'Dalaigh
Trans. John Montague

A Magic Mist

Through the deep night a magic mist led me
   like a simpleton roaming the land,
no friends of my bosom beside me,
   an outcast in places unknown.
I stretched out dejected and tearful
   in a nut-sheltered wood all alone
and prayed to the bright King of Glory
   with 'Mercy!' alone on my lips.

My heart, I declare, full of turmoil
   in that wood with no human sound nigh,
the thrush's sweet voice the sole pleasure,
   ever singing its tunes on each bough.
Then a noble *sidh-girl* sat beside me
   like a saint in her figure and form:
in her countenance roses contended
   with white – and I know not which lost.

Furrowed thick, yellow-twisting and golden
   was the lady's hair down to her shoes,
her brows without flaw, and like amber
   her luring eye, death to the brave.
Sweet, lovely, delicious – pure music –
   the harp-notes of the *sidh* from her lips,
breasts rounded, smooth, chalk-white, most proper,
   never marred by another, I swear.

Though lost to myself till that moment,
   with love for the lady I throbbed
and I found myself filled with great pleasure
   that she was directed my way.
How it fell, I write out in these verses,
   how I let my lips speak unrestrained,
the sweet things that I told the fair maiden
   as we stretched on the green mountain-slope:

'Are you, languid-eyed lady who pierced me
   with love for your face and your form,
the Fair-One caused hordes to be slaughtered
   as they write in the Battle of Troy?
Or the mild royal girl who let languish
   the chief of Boru and his troop?
Or the queen who decreed that the great prince
   from Howth follow far in pursuit?

Delicious, sweet, tender, she answered,
   ever shedding tears down in her pain:
'I am none of those women you speak of,
   and I see that you don't know my clan.
I'm the bride wed in bliss for a season,
   under right royal rule, to the King
over Caiseal of Conn and of Eoghan
   who ruled undisputed o'er Fódla.

'Gloomy my state, sad and mournful,
   by horned tyrants daily devoured,
and heavy oppressed by grim blackguards
   while my prince is set sailing abroad.
I look to the great Son of Glory
   to send my lion back to his sway
in his strong native towns, in good order,
   to flay the swarth goats with his blades.'

'Mild, golden-haired, courteous fair lady,
   of true royal blood, and no lie,
I mourn for your plight among blackguards,
   sad and joyless, dark under a pall.
If your King to his strong native mansions
   the Son of Glory should send, in His aid,
those swarth goats—swift, freely and willing—
   with shot would I joyfully flay!

'If our Stuart returned o'er the ocean
   to the lands of Inis Àilge in full course
with a fleet of Louis' men, and the Spaniard's,
   by dint of joy truly I'd be
on a prancing pure steed of swift mettle
   ever sluicing them out with much shot—
after which I'd not injure my spirit
   standing guard for the rest of my life.'

                    Eoghan Rua Ó Súilleabháin

Untitled

Brightness most bright I beheld on the way, forlorn.
Crystal of crystal her eye, blue touched with green.
Sweetness most sweet her voice, not stern with age.
Colour and pallor appeared in her flushed cheeks.

Curling and curling, each strand of her yellow hair
as it took the dew from the grass in its ample sweep;
a jewel more glittering than glass on her high bosom—
created, when she was created, in a higher world.

True tidings she revealed me, most forlorn,
tidings of one returning by royal right,
tidings of the crew ruined who drove him out,
and tidings I keep from my poem for sheer fear.

Foolish past folly, I came to her very presence
bound tightly, her prisoner (she likewise a prisoner . . .).
I invoked Mary's Son for succour: she started from me
and vanished like light to the fairy dwelling of Luachair.

Heart pounding, I ran, with a frantic haste in my race,
by the margins of marshes, through swamps, over bare moors.
To a powerful palace I came, by paths most strange,
to that place of all places, erected by druid magic.

All in derision they tittered - a gang of goblins
and a bevy of slender maidens with twining tresses.
They bound me in bonds, denying the slightest comfort,
and a lumbering brute took hold of my girl by the breasts.

I said to her then, in words that were full of truth,
how improper it was to join with that drawn gaunt creature
when a man the most fine, thrice over, of Scottish blood
was waiting to take her for his tender bride.

On hearing my voice she wept in high misery
and flowing tears fell down from her flushed cheeks.
She sent me a guard to guide me out of the palace -
that brightness most bright I beheld on the way, forlorn.

The Knot

Pain, disaster, downfall, sorrow and loss!
Our mild, bright, delicate, loving, fresh-lipped girl
with one of that black, horned, foreign, hate-crested crew
and no remedy near till our lions come over the sea.

Aogán Ó Rathaille

Kathaleen Ny-Houlahan

Long they pine in weary woe, the nobles of our land,
Long they wander to and fro, proscribed, alas! and banned;
Feastless, houseless, altarless, they bear the exile's brand,
But their hope is in the coming-to of Kathaleen Ny-Houlahan!

Think her not a ghastly hag, too hideous to be seen,
Call her not unseemly names, our matchless Kathaleen;
Young she is, and fair she is, and would be crowned a queen,
Were the king's son at home here with Kathaleen Ny-Houlahan!

Sweet and mild would look her face, O, none so sweet and mild,
Could she crush the foes by whom her beauty is reviled;
Woollen plaids would grace herself and robes of silk her child,
If the king's son were living here with Kathaleen Ny-Houlahan!

Sore disgrace it is to see the Arbitress of thrones,
Vassal to a *Saxoneen* of cold and sapless bones!
Bitter anguish wrings our souls – with heavy sighs and groans
We wait the Young Deliverer of Kathaleen Ny-Houlahan!

Let us pray to Him who holds Life's issues in His hands–
Him who formed the mighty globe, with all its thousand lands;
Girding them with seas and mountains, rivers deep, and strands,
To cast a look of pity upon Kathaleen Ny-Houlahan!

He, who over sands and waves led Israël along–
He, who fed, with heavenly bread, that chosen tribe and throng–
He, who stood by Moses, when his foes were fierce and strong–
May He show forth His might in saving Kathaleen Ny-Houlahan.

James Clarence Mangan

Dark Rosaleen

O my Dark Rosaleen,
    Do not sigh, do not weep!
The priests are on the ocean green,
    They march along the Deep.
There's wine . . . from the royal Pope
    Upon the ocean green;
And Spanish ale shall give you hope,
    My Dark Rosaleen!
    My own Rosaleen!
Shall glad your heart, shall give you hope,
Shall give you health, and help, and hope,
    My Dark Rosaleen.

Over hills and through dales,
    Have I roamed for your sake;
All yesterday I sailed with sails
    On river and on lake.
The Erne . . . at its highest flood
    I dashed across unseen,
For there was lightning in my blood,
    My Dark Rosaleen!
    My own Rosaleen!
Oh! there was lightning in my blood,
Red lightning lightened through my blood,
    My Dark Rosaleen!

All day long in unrest
    To and fro do I move,
The very soul within my breast
    Is wasted for you, love!
The heart . . . in my bosom faints
    To think of you, my Queen,
My life of life, my saint of saints,
    My Dark Rosaleen!
    My own Rosaleen!
To hear your sweet and sad complaints,
My life, my love, my saint of saints,
    My Dark Rosaleen!

Woe and pain, pain and woe,
    Are my lot night and noon,
To see your bright face clouded so,
    Like to the mournful moon.
But yet . . . will I rear your throne
    Again in golden sheen;

'Tis you shall reign, shall reign alone,
    My Dark Rosaleen!
    My own Rosaleen!
'Tis you shall have the golden throne,
'Tis you shall reign, and reign alone,
    My Dark Rosaleen!

Over dews, over sands
    Will I fly for your weal;
Your holy delicate white hands
    Shall girdle me with steel.
At home . . . in your emerald bowers,
    From morning's dawn till e'en,
You'll pray for me, my Flower of Flowers,
    My Dark Rosaleen!
    My fond Rosaleen!
You'll think of me through Daylight's hours,
My virgin flower, my Flower of Flowers,
    My Dark Rosaleen!

I could scale the blue air,
    I could plough the high hills,
Oh, I could kneel all night in prayer,
    To heal your many ills!
And one . . beamy smile from you
    Would float like light between
My toils and me, my own, my true,
    My Dark Rosaleen!
    My fond Rosaleen!
Would give me life and soul anew,
A second life, a soul anew,
    My Dark Rosaleen!

O! the Erne shall run red
    With redundance of blood,
The earth shall rock beneath our tread,
    And flames wrap hill and wood,
And gun-peal, and slogan cry,
    Wake many a glen serene,
Ere you shall fade, ere you shall die,
    My Dark Rosaleen!
    My own Rosaleen!
The Judgement Hour must first be nigh,
Ere you can fade, ere you can die,
    My Dark Rosaleen!

James Clarence Mangan

She Moved Through the Fair

My young love said to me, 'My brothers won't mind,
And my parents won't slight you for your lack of kind.'
Then she stepped away from me, and this she did say,
'It will not be long, love, till our wedding day.'

She stepped away from me and she moved through the fair,
And fondly I watched her go here and go there,
Then she went her way homeward with one star awake,
As the swan in the evening moves over the lake.

The people were saying no two were e'er wed
But one had a sorrow that never was said,
And I smiled as she passed with her goods and her gear,
And that was the last that I saw of my dear.

I dreamt it last night that my young love came in,
So softly she entered, her feet made no din;
She came close beside me, and this she did say,
'It will not be long, love, till our wedding day.'

Padraic Colum

Holyhead,
September 25, 1727

Lo here I sit at Holyhead
With muddy ale and mouldy bread:
All Christian victuals stink of fish,
I'm where my enemies would wish.
Convict of lies is every sign,
The inn has not one drop of wine.
I'm fastened both by wind and tide,
I see the ship at anchor ride.
The captain swears the sea's too rough,
He has not passengers enough.
And thus the Dean is forced to stay,
Till others come to help the pay.
In Dublin they'd be glad to see
A packet though it brings in me.
They cannot say the winds are cross;
Your politicians at a loss
For want of matter swears and frets,
Are forced to read the old gazettes.
I never was in haste before
To reach that slavish hateful shore:
Before, I always found the wind
To me was most malicious kind,
But now the danger of a friend
On whom my hopes and fears depend,
Absent from whom all climes are cursed,
With whom I'm happy in the worst,
With rage impatient makes me wait
A passage to the land I hate.
Else, rather on this bleaky shore
Where loudest winds incessant roar,
Where neither herb nor tree will thrive,
Where nature hardly seems alive,
I'd go in freedom to my grave,
Than rule yon isle and be slave.

                                    Jonathan Swift

On Dreams
An Imitation of Petronius

Those Dreams that on the silent Night intrude,
And with false flitting Shades our Minds delude,
Jove never sends us downward from the Skies,
Nor can they from infernal Mansions rise;
But all are meer Productions of the Brain,
And Fools consult Interpreters in vain.

For, when in Bed we rest our weary Limbs,
The Mind unburthen'd sports in various Whims,
The busy Head with mimick Art runs o'er
The Scenes and Actions of the Day before.

The drowsy Tyrant, by his Minions led,
To regal Rage devotes some Patriot's Head.
With equal Terrors, not with equal Guilt,
The Murderer dreams of all the Blood he spilt.

The Soldier smiling hears the Widow's Cries,
And stabs the Son before the Mother's Eyes.
With like Remorse his Brother of the Trade,
The Butcher, feels the Lamb beneath his blade.

The Statesman rakes the Town to find a Plot,
And dream of Forfeitures by Treason got.
Nor less Tom Turd-Man of true Statesman mold,
Collects the City Filth in search of Gold.

Orphans around his Bed the Lawyer sees,
And takes the Plaintiff's and Defendant's Fees.
His Fellow Pick-Purse, watching for a Job,
Fancies his Fingers in the Cully's Fob.

The kind Physician grants the Husband's Prayers,
Or gives Relief to long-expecting Heirs.
The sleeping Hangman ties the fatal Noose,
Nor unsuccessful waits for dead Men's Shoes.

The grave Divine with knotty Points perplext,
As if he were awake, nods o'er his Text:
While the sly Mountebank attends his Trade,
Harangues the Rabble, and is better paid.

The hireling Senator of modern Days,
Bedaubs the guilty Great with nauseous Praise:
And Dick the Scavenger with equal Grace,
Flirts from his Cart the Mud in *Walpole's* Face.

Jonathan Swift

The Man Upright

I once spent an evening in a village
Where the people are all taken up with tillage,
Or do some business in a small way
Among themselves, and all the day
Go crooked, doubled to half their size,
Both working and loafing, with their eyes
Stuck in the ground or in a board,–
For some of them tailor, and some of them hoard
Pence in a till in their little shops,
And some of them shoe-soles – they get the tops
Ready-made from England, and they die cobblers–
All bent up double, a village of hobblers
And slouchers and squatters, whether they straggle
Up and down, or bend to haggle
Over a counter, or bend at a plough,
Or to dig with a spade, or to milk a cow,
Or to shove the goose-iron stiffly along
The stuff on the sleeve-board, or lace the fong
In the boot on the last, or to draw the wax-end
Tight cross-ways – and so to make or to mend
What will soon be worn out by the crooked people.
The only thing straight in the place was the steeple,
I thought at first. I was wrong in that;
For there past the window at which I sat
Watching the crooked little men
Go slouching, and with the gait of a hen
An odd little woman go pattering past,
And the cobbler crouching over his last
In his window opposite, and next door
The tailor squatting inside on the floor–
While I watched them, as I have said before,
And thought that only the steeple was straight,
There came a man of a different gait–
A man who neither slouched nor pattered,
But planted his steps as if each step mattered;
Yet walked down the middle of the street
Not like a policeman on his beat,
But like man with nothing to do
Except walk straight upright like me and you.

Thomas MacDonagh

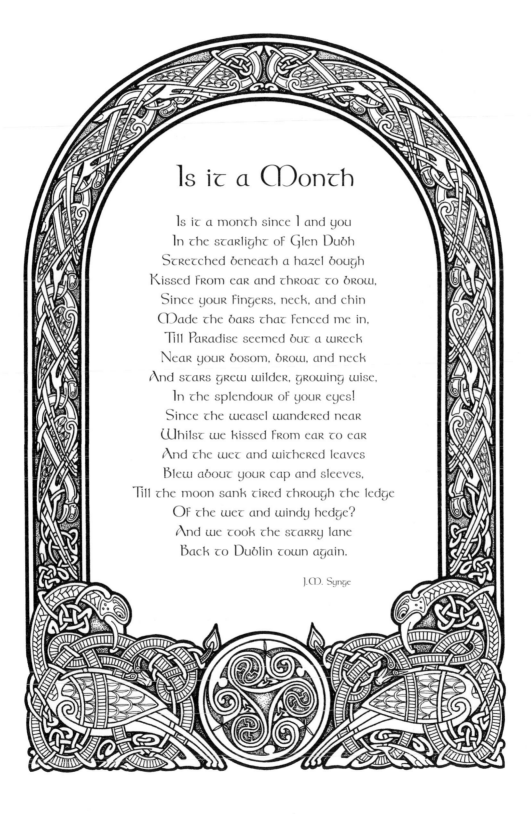

Is it a Month

Is it a month since I and you
In the starlight of Glen Dubh
Stretched beneath a hazel bough
Kissed from ear and throat to brow,
Since your fingers, neck, and chin
Made the bars that fenced me in,
Till Paradise seemed but a wreck
Near your bosom, brow, and neck
And stars grew wilder, growing wise,
In the splendour of your eyes!
Since the weasel wandered near
Whilst we kissed from ear to ear
And the wet and withered leaves
Blew about your cap and sleeves,
Till the moon sank tired through the ledge
Of the wet and windy hedge?
And we took the starry lane
Back to Dublin town again.

J.M. Synge

The Vision

One morning ere Titan had thought to stir his feet,
on the top of a fine high hill I had laboured up,
I chanced on a pleasant flock of joyous girls,
a troop from Sidh Seanadh's bright mansions to the north.

A film of enchantment spread, of aspect bright,
from the shining boulders of Galway to Cork of the harbours:
clusters of fruit appearing in every treetop,
acorns in woods, pure honey upon the stones.

Three candles they lit, of indescribable light,
on Cnoc Firinne's lofty summit in Conallach Rua.
Then I followed the flock of cloaked women as far as Thomond
and questioned them on their diligent round of tasks.

Then answered the lady Aoibhill, of aspect bright,
they had cause to light three candles above the harbours:
in the name of the faithful king who is soon to come
to rule and defend the triple realm for ever.

I started up - soft, sudden-out of my dream
believing the good news Aoibhill told me was true,
but found that I was nerve-shaken, downcast and morose
that morning ere Titan had thought to stir his feet.

Aogan Ó Rathaille

On Freedom and Ambition

Ye powers of truth, that did my soul aspire,
Far from my bosom drive the low desire:
And thou, fair Freedom, taught alike to feel
The rabble's rage, and tyrant's angry steel:
Thou transitory flower, alike undone
By proud contempt, or favour's fostering sun,
Still may thy blooms the changeful clime endure,
I only would repress them to secure:
For just experience tells, in every soil,
That those who think must govern those that toil;
And all that Freedom's highest aims can reach,
Is but to lay proportion'd loads on each.
Hence, should one order disproportion'd grow,
Its double weight must ruin all below.

O then how blind to all that truth requires,
Who think it freedom when a part aspires!
Calm is my soul, nor apt to rise in arms,
Except when fast-approaching danger warms:
But when contending chiefs blockade the throne,
Contracting regal power to stretch their own;
When I behold a factious band agree
To call it freedom when themselves are free;
Each wanton judge new penal statutes draw,
Laws grind the poor, and rich men rule the law;
The wealth of climes, where savage nations roam,
Pillag'd from slaves to purchase slaves at home;
Fear, pity, justice, indignation start,
Tear off reserve, and bare my swelling heart;
Till half a patriot, half a coward grown,
I fly from petty tyrants to the throne.

Yes, brother, curse with me that baleful hour,
When first ambition struck at regal power;
And thus polluting honour in its source,
Gave wealth to sway the mind with double force.
Have we not seen, round Britain's peopled shore,
Her useful sons exchang'd for useless ore?
Seen all her triumphs but destruction haste,
Like flaring tapers bright'ning as they waste;
Seen opulence, her grandeur to maintain,
Lead stern depopulation in her train,
And over fields where scatter'd hamlets rose,

In barren solitary pomp repose?
Have we not seen, at pleasure's lordly call,
The smiling long-frequented village fall?
Beheld the duteous son, the sire decay'd,
The modest matron, and the blushing maid,
Forc'd from their homes, a melancholy train,
To traverse climes beyond the western main;
Where wild Oswego spreads her swamps around,
And Niagara stuns with thund'ring sound?

E'en now, perhaps, as there some pilgrim strays
Through tangled forests, and through dangerous ways;
Where beasts with man divided empire claim,
And the brown Indian marks with murd'rous aim;
There, while above the giddy tempest flies,
And all around distressful yells arise,
The pensive exile, bending with his woe,
To stop too fearful, and too faint to go,
Casts a long look where England's glories shine,
And bids his bosom sympathise with mine.

Vain, very vain, my weary search to find
That bliss which only centres in the mind:
Why have I stray'd from pleasure and repose,
To seek a good each government bestows?
In every government, though terrors reign,
Though tyrant kings, or tyrant laws restrain,
How small, of all that human hearts endure,
That part which laws or kings can cause or cure.
Still to ourselves in every place consign'd,
Our own felicity we make or find:
With secret course, which no loud storms annoy,
Glides the smooth current of domestic joy.
The lifted axe, the agonising wheel,
Luke's iron crown, and Damien's bed of steel,
To men remote from power but rarely known,
Leave reason, faith, and conscience, all our own.

Oliver Goldsmith

The Eviction

In early morning twighlight, raw and chill,
Damp vapours brooding on the barren hill,
Through miles of mire in steady grave array
Threescore well-arm'd police pursue their way;
Each tall and bearded man a rifle swings,
And under each greatcoat a bayonet clings;
The Sheriff on his sturdy cob astride
Talks with the chief, who marches by their side,
And, creeping on behind them, Paudeen Dhu
Pretends his needful duty much to rue.
Six big-boned labourers, clad in common frieze,
Walk in the midst, the Sheriff's staunch allies;
Six crowbar men, from distant county brought,-
Orange, and glorying in their work, 'tis thought,
But wrongly, - churls of Catholics are they,
And merely hired at half-a-crown a day.

The Hamlet clustering on its hill is seen,
A score of petty homesteads, dark and mean;
Poor always, not despairing until now;
Long used, as well as poverty knows how,
With life's oppressive trifles to contend.
This day will bring its history to an end.
Moveless and grim against the cottage walls
Lean a few silent men: but someone calls
Far off; and then a child without a stitch
Runs out of doors, flies back with piercing screech,
And soon from house to house is heard the cry
Of female sorrow, swelling loud and high,
Which makes the men blaspheme between their teeth.
Meanwhile, o'er fence and watery field beneath,
The little army moves through drizzling rain;
A 'Crowbar' leads the Sheriff's nag; the lane
Is enter'd, and their plashing tramp draws near;
One instant, outcry holds its breath to hear;
'Halt!' - at the doors they form in double line,
And ranks of polish'd rifles wetly shine.

The Sheriff's painful duty must be done;
He begs for quiet - and the work's begun.
The strong stand ready; now appear the rest,
Girl, matron, grandsire, baby on the breast,
And Rosy's thin face on a pallet borne;
A motley concourse, feeble and forlorn.
One old man, tears upon his wrinkled cheek,

Stands trembling on a threshold, tries to speak,
But, in defect of any word for this,
Mutely upon the doorpost prints a kiss,
Then passes out for ever. Through the crowd
The children run bewilder'd, wailing loud;
Where needed most, the men combine their aid;
And, least of all, is Oona forth convey'd,
Reclined in her accustom'd strawen chair,
Her aged eyelids closed, her thick white hair
Escaping from her cap; she feels the chill,
Looks round and murmurs, then again is still.

Now bring the remnants of each household fire.
On the wet grounds the hissing coals expire;
And Paudeen Dhu, with meekly dismal face,
Receives the full possession of the place.

Whereon the Sheriff, 'We have legal hold.
Return to shelter with the sick and old.
Time shall be given; and there are carts below
If any to the workhouse choose to go.'
A young man makes him answer, grave and clear,
'We're thankful to you! but there's no one here
Goin' back into them houses: do your part.
Nor we won't trouble Pigot's horse and cart.'
At which name, rushing into th' open space,
A woman flings her hood from off her face,
Falls on her knees upon the miry ground,
Lifts hands and eyes, and voice of thrilling sound,-
'Vengeance of God Almighty fall on you,
James Pigot! - may the poor man's curse pursue,
The widow's and the orphan's curse, I pray,
Hang heavy round you at your dying day!'
Breathless and fix'd one moment stands the crowd
To hear this malediction fierce and loud.

But now (our neighbour Neal is busy there)
On steady poles he lifted Oona's chair,
Well-heap'd with borrow'd mantles; gently bear
The sick girl in her litter, bed and all;
Whilst others hug the children weak and small
In careful arms, or hoist them pick-a-back;
And, 'midst the unrelenting clink and thwack
Of iron bar on stone, let creep away
The sad procession from that hill-side grey,
Through the slow-falling rain. In three hours more
You find, where Ballytullagh stood before,
Mere shatter'd walls, and doors with useless latch,
And firesides buried under fallen thatch.

William Allingham

From
The Deserted Village

Sweet smiling village, loveliest of the lawn,
Thy sports are fled, and all thy charms withdrawn;
Amidst thy bowers the tyrant's hand is seen,
And desolation saddens all thy green:
One only master grasps the whole domain,
And half a tillage stints thy smiling plain:
No more thy glassy brook reflects the day,
But choked with sedges, works its weedy way;
Along thy glades, a solitary guest,
The hollow-sounding bittern guards its nest;
Amidst thy desert walks the lapwing flies,
And tires their echoes with unvaried cries.
Sunk are thy bowers in shapeless ruin all,
And the long grass o'ertops the mouldering wall,
And, trembling, shrinking from the spoiler's hand,
Far, far away, thy children leave the land.

Ill fares the land, to hastening ills a prey,
Where wealth accumulates, and men decay,
Princes and lords may flourish, or may fade;
A breath can make them, as a breath has made;
But a bold peasantry, their country's pride,
When once destroyed, can never be supplied.

A time there was, ere England's griefs began,
When every rood of ground maintained its man;
For him light labour spread her wholesome store,
Just gave what life required, but gave no more:
His best companions, innocence and health;
And his best riches, ignorance of wealth.

But times are altered; Trade's unfeeling train
Usurp the land and dispossess the swain;
Along the lawn, where scattered hamlets rose,
Unwieldy wealth, and cumbrous pomp repose;
And every want to opulence allied,
And every pang that folly pays to pride.
These gentle hours that plenty bade to bloom,
Those calm desires that asked but little room,
Those healthful sports that graced the peaceful scene,
Lived in each look, and brightened all the green;
These far departing seek a kinder shore,
And rural mirth and manners are no more.

Oliver Goldsmith

Lament for Thomas Davis

I walked through Ballinderry in the spring-time,
　　When the bud was on the tree;
And I said, in every fresh-ploughed field beholding
　　The sowers striding free,
Scattering broadside forth the corn in golden plenty
　　On the quick seed-clasping soil:
'Even such, this day, among the fresh-stirred hearts of Erin,
　　Thomas Davis, is thy toil!'

I sat by Ballyshannon in the summer,
　　And saw the salmon leap;
And I said, as I beheld the gallant creatures
　　Spring glittering from the deep,
Through the spray, and through the prone heaps striving onward
　　To the calm clear streams above,
'So seekest thou thy native founts of freedom, Thomas Davis,
　　In thy brightest of strength and love!'

I stood on Derrybawn in the autumn,
　　And I heard the eagle call,
With a clangorous cry of wrath and lamentation
　　That filled the wide mountain hall,
Over the bare deserted place of his plundered eyrie;
　　And I said, as he screamed and soared,
'So callest thou, thou wrathful soaring Thomas Davis,
　　For a nation's rights restored!'

And alas! to think but now, and thou art lying,
　　Dear Davis, dead at thy mother's knee;
And I, no mother near, on my own sick-bed,
　　That face on earth shall never see;
I may lie and try to feel that I am dreaming,
　　I may lie and try to say, 'Thy will be done'-
But a hundred such as I will never comfort Erin
　　For the loss of the noble son!

Young husbandman of Erin's fruitful seed-time,
　　In the fresh track of danger's plough!
Who will walk the heavy, toilsome, perilous furrow
　　Girt with freedom's seed-sheets now?

Who will banish with the wholesome crop of knowledge
    The daunting weed and the bitter thorn,
Now that thou thyself art but a seed for hopeful planting
    Against the Resurrection morn?

Young salmon of the flood-tide of freedom
    That swells round Erin's shore!
Thou wilt leap against their loud oppressive torrent
    Of bigotry and hate no more;
Drawn downward by their prone material instinct,
    Let them thunder on their rocks and foam—
Thou hast leapt, aspiring soul, to founts beyond their raging,
    Where troubled waters never come!

But I grieve not, Eagle of the empty eyrie,
    That thy wrathful cry is still;
And that the songs alone of peaceful mourners
    Are heard today on Erin's hill;
Better far, if brothers' war be destined for us
    (God avert that horrid day, I pray),
That ere our hands be stained with slaughter fratricidal
    Thy warm heart should be cold in clay.

But my trust is strong in God, who made us brothers,
    That He will not suffer their right hands
Which thou hast joined in holier rites than wedlock
    To draw opposing brands.
Oh, many a tuneful tongue that thou mad'st vocal
    Would lie cold and silent then;
And songless long once more, should often-widowed Erin
    Mourn the loss of her brave young men.

Oh, brave young men, my love, my pride, my promise,
    'Tis on you my hopes are set,
In manliness, in kindliness, in justice,
    To make Erin a nation yet,
Self-respecting, self-relying, self-advancing,
    In union or in severance, free and strong—
And if God grant this, then, under God, to Thomas Davis
    Let the greater praise belong.

Samuel Ferguson

The Rebel

I am come of the seed of the people, the people that sorrow,
That have no treasure but hope,
No riches laid up but a memory
Of an Ancient glory.
My mother bore me in bondage, in bondage my mother was born,
I am of the blood of serfs;
The children with whom I have played, the men and women with whom I have eaten,
Have had masters over them, have been under the lash of masters,
And, though gentle, have served churls;
The hands that have touched mine, the dear hands whose touch is familiar to me,
Have worn shameful manacles, have been bitten at the wrist by manacles,
Have grown hard with the manacles and the task-work of strangers,
I am flesh of the flesh of these lowly, I am bone of their bone,
I that have never submitted;
I that have a soul greater than the souls of my people's masters,
I that have vision and prophecy and the gift of fiery speech,
I that have spoken with God on the top of His holy hill.

And because I am of the people, I understand the people,
I am sorrowful with their sorrow, I am hungry with their desire:
My heart has been heavy with the grief of mothers,
My eyes have been wet with the tears of children,
I have yearned with old wistful men,
And laughed or cursed with young men;
Their shame is my shame, and I have reddened for it,
Reddened for that they have served, they who should be free,
Reddened for that they have gone in want, while others have been full,
Reddened for that they have walked in fear of lawyers and of their jailors
With their writs of summons and their handcuffs,
Men mean and cruel!
I could have borne stripes on my body rather than this shame of my people.

And now I speak, being full of vision;
I speak to my people, and I speak in my people's name to the masters of my people.
I say to my people that they are holy, that they are august, despite their chains,
That they are greater than those that hold them, and stronger and purer,
That they have but need of courage, and to call on the name of their God,
God the unforgetting, the dear God that loves the peoples
For whom He died naked, suffering shame.
And I say to my people's masters: Beware,
Beware of the thing that is coming, beware of the risen people,
Who shall take what ye would not give. Did ye think to conquer the people,
Or that Law is stronger than life and than men's desire to be free?
We will try it out with you, ye that have harried and held,
Ye that have bullied and bribed, tyrants, hypocrites, liars!

Patrick Pearse

Prayer Before Birth

I am not yet born; O hear me.
Let not the bloodsucking bat or the rat or the stoat or the
    club-footed ghoul come near me.

I am not yet born, console me.
I fear that the human race may with tall walls wall me,
    with strong drugs dope me, with wise lies lure me,
        on black racks rack me, in blood-baths roll me.

I am not yet born; provide me
With water to dandle me, grass to grow for me, trees to talk
    to me, sky to sing to me, birds and a white light
        in the back of my mind to guide me.

I am not yet born; forgive me
For the sins that in me the world shall commit, my words
    when they speak me, my thoughts when they think me,
        my treason engendered by traitors beyond me,
          my life when they murder by means of my
            hands, my death when they live me.

I am not yet born; rehearse me
In the parts I must play and the cues I must take when
    old men lecture me, bureaucrats hector me, mountains
        frown at me, lovers laugh at me, the white
          waves call me to folly and the desert calls
            me to doom and the beggar refuses
              my gift and my children curse me.

I am not yet born; O hear me,
Let not the man who is beast or who thinks he is God
        come near me.

I am not yet born; O fill me
With strength against those who would freeze my
        humanity, would dragoon me into a lethal automaton,
            would make me a cog in a machine, a thing with
                one face, a thing, and against all those
                    who would dissipate my entirety, would
                        blow me like thistledown hither and
                            thither or hither and thither
                                like water held in the
                                    hands would spill me.

Let them not make me a stone and let them not spill me.
Otherwise kill me.

                                            Louis MacNeice

Appendix A

Pronunciation Guide

As mentioned already there are a great number of versions for the spelling of people and place names. I have also encountered some discrepancies in pronunciation of these. The most pleasing guide to pronunciation I have found was Thomas Kinsella's notes in his translation of *The Táin* and, with his permission, I have largely used those here. Having said that, this is still only a rough guide and variations will still occur. It is worth familiarizing yourself with as many of the words as possible, as in English they lose much of their lyrical quality and detract from the poems themselves. Also, when written phonetically in English they seem to lose their strength, they need to be seen in Irish.

Consonants

Consonants at the beginning of a word are the same as in English except for c which is always pronounced as a k. Elsewhere

> b = v
> c = g or k
> ch = a guttural sound as in 'loch'
> d = dh as in 'then'
> g = gh soft guttural or silent
> m = v
> t = d
> s followed or preceded by e or i = sh
> th = th as in thin

Vowels

An accent over a vowel indicates length and are pronounced awe, ay, ee, owe, oo (e.g. dún is doon)

> ai = a in the first syllable (Ailill) and i elsewhere (Cúchulainn)
> a final e is sounded
> iu = u with the i slightly sounded (Derdriu)
> ui = i with the u slightly sounded
> ei = e (murtheimne)

Pronunciation of key words (bold type indicates stressed syllables)

> Aife: **ee** - fe
> Ailill: **al** - il
> Amairgin: **av** - ar - ghin
> Badb: badhv /bive
> Caoilte : kweel - tya
> Conchobor: **kon** - chov - or / **kon** - chor
> Cúchulainn: koo - ch**ull** - in
> Cuailnge: **koo** - ling - e

Derdriu: **der** - dru
Emain Macha: **ev** - in **ma** - cha
Eochaid: (y)**och** - i
Fedelm: fedh - elm
Ferdia: fer - **di** - a
Finnabair: **fin** - av - ir
Medb: medhv / mayv
Morrígan: **mo** - ree - ghan
Murtheimne: **mur** - thev - ne
Noisiu: **noy** - shu
Scáthach: **skaw** - thach
Sídhe: shee
Sliab: **shlee** - av
Sualdam: **soo** - al - dav
Táin: toyn
Uisliu: **ish** - lu

Appendix B

Explanatory notes for some of the mythological poems in 'The Mists of Time'

Amairgin's Song of Ireland *(see p.23)*
The sea-born invading Milesians (Gaelic Celts) are held beyond the ninth wave, offshore to the west of Ireland, by a storm created by the Tuatha de Danaan's druid's magic. On-board Amairgin White-Knee, a Milesian shaman and poet, invokes properties and features within the land of Ireland by his song, and aids the Milesians' approach. The storm calms immediately and, with the Milesians' arrival, a new age is upon Ireland.

TARA – the ancient seat of the kings of Ireland. In myth it was originally the capital of the Tuatha De Danaan. In actuality it was in use before the Celts arrived in Ireland, and featured in many Irish legends.

EIRE – Eriu was one of the three Danaan goddesses of the land that Amairgin petitioned on his first arrival in Ireland before being tricked into agreeing to go beyond the ninth wave. He promised all three that their names should be a name for Ireland. Eriu's name stayed after she in turn promised the land would belong to the invading Milesians for ever.

EREMON – the king of all Ireland after the Milesian invasion.

The Lay of Fintan *(see p.24)*
This recounts the six waves of invasions of Ireland which resulted in the arrival of the Milesians. Its major telling is in the twelfth-century *Lebor Gabala Erenn* (*The Book of Conquests*). Fintan is the sole survivor of the first wave and, through shapeshifting into different animals, he passed through the centuries observing the different invasions, before re-emerging once more in human form. *The Book of Conquests* in its twelfth-century form may well have been an interpretation of the passage from a pagan to a Christian Ireland. In it, the undoubtedly pagan Tuatha De Danaan, though possessing many fine qualities, could not be the precursors of that Christian Ireland. The arrival of the Milesians was the catalyst that prepared the race for conversion. The Milesians were given antecedents of biblical status to make their presence even more legitimate.

THE SIX INVASIONS – Cessair led the first invasion. She was the daughter of Bith, who was the son of Noah of biblical fame. Her company consisted of herself, fifty women and three men including Fintan. All were wiped out in the biblical flood except Fintan.

A race called the Fomorians inhabited Ireland until the second invasion, led by Parthalon, forced them out. During their stay the Parthalonians changed the shape of the land by adding plains and lakes. Until their arrival, Ireland had one plain and three lakes. Plague wiped out all but one Parthelonian, leading to the third invasion.

Nemed led this invasion. Again his people changed some of the features of Ireland adding some more rivers, lakes and plains. After the death of

Nemed, the Fomorians were able to return, oppressing the Nemedians until they had no option but to rebel. Failing to retake the land, the remaining Nemedians (a single boatload) were forced to flee. Settling in other lands, some in Greece, others to the north, their descendants led the next two invasions.

Those settling in Greece had split into three races: the Fir Bolg, the Fir Galion and the Fir Domnann. They comprised the fourth invasion, dominated by the Fir Bolg, and between them Ireland was divided into the five provinces of Ulster, Leinster, Munster, Connacht and Meath.

The northerly remnant of the Nemedians became the afore-mentioned Tuatha De Danaan, who had become elevated to the status of gods (though later writings reduced them to the role of fairies and, worse, leprechauns). Sweeping in on a magic cloud the Tuatha De Danaan led the fifth invasion, defeating both the Fir Bolg and the Fomorians in separate battles.

Lastly came the sons of Míl or Milesians and the invasion cycle is complete.

The Hosting of the Sidhe *(see p.26)*

The Sidhe were what the Tuatha De Danaan became in folkloric terms after they withdrew to the Otherworld (The Land of Youth) following the Milesian invasion and the agreement that the land should be split between them – the Milesians in the world above, the De Danaan the world below. *Sidhe* is also the Gaelic for wind and the wind can sometimes signify the presence of the Sidhe.

NIAMH – the daughter of a king of the Sidhe in the Land of Youth who lured Ossian, son of Fionn Mac Cumhaill, there – see also 'The Praise of Fionn'.

KNOCKNAREA – a mountain in county Sligo.

The Land Oversea *(see p.27)*

This refers to the Land of Youth, one of many names for the home of the Tuatha De Danaan. Also known as the Land of the Dead, in Irish it is *Tir Na Og*. This poem is sung by Niamh to lure Ossian away.

The Praise of Fionn *(see p.28)*

Having been lured away by Niamh for what he thought was a week, but turned out to be 300 years, Ossian returned to Ireland from the Land of Youth to find that his father Fionn and the elite warriors of the Fianna had been long forgotten. It was now a land where St Patrick and his followers held sway, and the old ways were gone. On returning, Ossian still had the glamour of the Otherworld upon him but when he dismounted from his horse and touched the actual land, his bond with the past was re-made and he was transformed into a withered old man, in keeping with his true age. It was then that he was taken to St Patrick where he recounted the exploits and times of Fionn and the Fianna.

Caoilte *(see p.30)*
Caoilte was another member of the Fianna and a compatriot of Ossian. He is said to have lived to such a great age that he also met St Patrick and told him of Fionn and the Fianna after being baptized into Christianity.

OSGAR (OSCAR) – the son of Ossian and hence the grandson of Fionn.

DIARMUID – a member of the Fianna, later hunted down by Fionn after he was forced by honour to help Fionn's wife-to-be, Grania, escape a marriage she did not want. This has echoes of themes found later in 'Derdrie's Lament' and 'Derdriu's Reply' and is briefly touched upon in the poem 'The Celts'.

The Wooing of Etain *(see p.42)*
Etain was the second wife of the Danaan prince, Midir. Through the magic of a jealous first wife, she was transformed into a mortal child, unaware of her true Danaan nature. Her great beauty (she was reported as being the fairest maid in all of Ireland) drew the attention of the high king Eochaid, who persuaded her to be his wife at Tara. Eventually, Midir discovered her whereabouts and attempted to persuade her back to the Land of Youth, their original home, of which she still had no knowledge.

The Song of Wandering Aengus *(see p.43)*
Aengus was the son of the Dagda one of the chief gods of the Tuatha De Danaan, and was the Irish god of love. His foster father was Midir whom he helped in the wooing of Etain the first time round, before her transformation to a mortal. He also helped Dairmuid and Grania escape many times from the pursuing Fionn.

Fergus and the Druid *(see p.44)*
Fergus mac Roy was the king of Ulster but Nessa, whom he loved, asked that her son by another, Conchobor (Conchubar), could be king for a year in order that his descendants would be that of a king. Fergus agreed to this. However, once a year had passed Conchobor remained king, as due to Nessa's machinations the people of Ulster preferred him. Fergus's love of feasting and the hunt, rather than the ardours of kingship, meant he did not object to this situation. He stayed in the court of Ulster at Emain Macha until events took a turn for the worse for him and then the whole of Ulster.

Deirdre's Lament for the Sons of Usnach/Derdriu's Reply *(see p.46-9)*
These two poems are linked as they deal with the same story but are from different sources. This highlights the problem with the many forms of spelling that occur in the accounts of early Irish myths. In these two poems Deirdre/Derdriu, Neesa/Noisiu, Usnach/Uisliu and Conor/Conchobor are the same people. For these notes I am using the second versions from Thomas Kinsella's translation of *The Táin* simply because I think they sound better.

Conchobor had kept the girl Derdriu isolated until she was old enough to marry him. It had been prophesied at her birth that through her great beauty much harm would be done to Ulster and many advised to have her

killed. Conchobor wanted her for himself and decided that if no one saw her, the prophesied evil could be avoided. Understandably, Derdriu was not content with this arrangement and she sought another. It was to Noisiu, son of Uisliu and one of Conchobor's warriors, that she turned. He was more to her liking than Conchobor, by then an old man. Through threat of shame and mockery, Derdriu forced Noisiu and his brothers to take her away. They became hunted exiles for many years, first in Ireland then over the sea in Alba (Scotland). They never found true rest, but lived in contentment in the wilder places. Finally Conchobor sent Noisiu's friend Fergus mac Roy with promises of forgiveness if they returned, since it was said that men of Ulster should not have to hide in a foreign land. As Fergus was well respected and trusted, they returned. Conchobor, however, intended to deceive Noisiu and deliberately delayed an unwitting Fergus on the return journey. Thinking all was well, the sons of Uisliu returned to Emain Macha with Fergus's own son. There, using others to keep his hands clean, Conchobor had everyone but Derdriu killed. The result was that Fergus sought revenge for the way he had been used in the betrayal and the death of his son and his friends, the sons of Uisliu. Many were killed including Conchobor's son. Fergus went into self-imposed exile, taking his followers with him to neighbouring Connacht, not normally a haven for Ulstermen, where Ailill and Medb ruled. Derdriu was kept in confinement for a year by Conchobor. When he tried to soothe her, she answered with the poem 'Derdriu's Reply'. Finally, being transported away by Conchobor whose patience was wearing thin, she leapt from a carriage and dashed her brains on a rock.

This was the main precursor to the story of the Táin Bo Cuailnge or Cattle Raid of Cooley. In the province of Connacht, Ailill and Medb argued about which of them was the more wealthy. Much to their annoyance, they were equal in all things, including jewellery, fine cloth, land, slaves and live-stock. But there was one thing in which they differed: Ailill had a bull, Finnbennach the white-horned, that Medb could not match. Its equal could only be found in Ulster. The brown bull of Cuailnge was called Donn Cuailnge and its connection with Finnbennach was that both were the reincarnations of two rivalling stockmen. Medb negotiated for a year to obtain the bull in order to match her husband's, but she failed when one of her team drunkenly let slip that if the negotiations did fall through, they would take the bull by force. The minor chieftain on whose land the bull grazed had, until that point, been willing to agree, but now he sent the emissaries away. For Medb, the only answer was war. Medb called in the aid of the other three provinces, and along with Fergus and his men, it was Ulster against the rest of Ireland.

Fedelm's Prophesy (see p.50)
As the assembled armies of the four provinces marched, they encountered Fedelm, a Connacht poetess returning from spiritual training in Alba. She had the power of foresight and, expecting a good outcome, Medb implored Fedelm to use her talent. The result was not to Medb's liking.

CÚCHULAINN – the champion of Ulster and foster son of Fergus mac Roy. Also known as the Hound of Ulster or Culann's hound, after an episode when, as a young boy, he had killed the guard dog of the smith Culann and had promised to take on the role of guard dog. This was to be until he had trained a new one as good as the one he had killed. Even from a young age, he was a most formidable warrior, learning and becoming proficient in all arts of war. When it became obvious he could teach himself no more, he was sent for further training in Alba under the tutorage of the female warrior Scáthach. Here the final weapon she taught him to use was the *gea bolga*. This was a weapon hurled with the foot and on entering the body filled every part with lethal barbs. Cúchulainn was the first champion that Scáthach considered worthy enough to train in its use. Cúchulainn also had a secret fighting strategy at his disposal, and this was his tendency, while fighting, to undergo what is called warp-spasm. When this occurred his body would seriously contort out of shape and his strength was increased many fold. It was a process akin to that of a whirling dervish, and made him a far more dangerous opponent. It was Cúchulainn alone among the men of Ulster, being of partial De Danaan blood, who did not suffer from the Curse of Macha. This curse decreed that at a time of peril to Ulster, the menfolk of that province should be debilitated by the pains of childbirth for a number of days. This was why, when Ailill and Medb raised the armies of Ireland against Ulster, it was Cúchulainn alone who stood against them until the rest of Ulster rose from its pangs.

The Morrígan *(see p.52)*
The Morrígan is the triple aspect goddess of war, sexuality and death who sometimes takes on the form of a crow. She does so here while Cúchulainn is holding off the armies of Ailill and Medb and alights on a stone next to Donn Cuailnge, the brown bull, telling it of the slaughter to come in its name.

The Charioteer's Chant *(see p.53)*
Cúchulainn had successfully held off the assembled armies causing great loss of life. Appalled at this, Medb and Ailill persuaded Cúchulainn to take on the Champions of Ireland in single handed combat. For the duration of this combat the armies of Ireland could advance into Ulster. If Cúchulainn was victorious the armies had to halt until the next day when another champion would be sent out. The combats were inevitably short, despite some attempts at treachery by Medb, and little advance was made. Meanwhile, the end of the childbearing pangs (see **Fedelm's Prophecy** above) of the men of Ulster grew nearer. Understandably, Medb was experiencing difficulties in finding warriors ready to take up the challenge. As an incentive she offered her daughter, Finnabair, in marriage to a returning champion. Still they died. At last it was the turn of Ferdia mac Damáin to be persuaded. He was Cúchulainn's foster brother. They had both trained with Scáthach in Alba, where they swore to be life-long friends. Many inducements were offered to Ferdia, including Finnabair, but Ferdia declined, not wanting to fight his much-loved foster brother. Once more, Medb used deception, as she had done many times

before in this campaign, by claiming Cúchulainn had said that to defeat Ferdia would be unimportant and no great achievement. Incensed by this, Ferdia took all Medb's offers and vowed to set out the next morning against Cúchulainn. Hearing this, Fergus mac Roy left the camp of the host of Ireland to warn Cúchulainn. The next morning, while Ferdia rested, his charioteer spied the approach of Cúchulainn and, waking his master, made his chant.

Cúchulainn's Lament (see p.54)
The two champions met. They fought over a series of days, one of them choosing the particular weapons to be used on each day. At the end of the first day's fighting they parted, still as friends, embracing one another. Their charioteers sat around the same campfire and horses shared the same stabling. The two champions shared food and healing herbs to repair the many wounds of the day's fighting, so that neither should have the advantage the next day through having had greater sustenance and healing. The fighting continued, each champion performing great battle feats. Such is the way of the Celtic warrior, being well versed in the use of many weapons. With the passing of each day, however, they grew more weary. Their wounds became intense, their charioteers no longer shared the same fire, and their horses separated. On the last morning, fearing the *gea bolga*, Ferdia wore many layers of armour to protect himself from this fearful weapon. When the time came, it was not enough. Himself sorely wounded, Cúchulainn had no choice but to use the *gea bolga*. He hurled it with his foot such that it ripped through iron and stone, tearing into Ferdias body and causing fatal damage.

AIFE – a female warrior rival to Scáthach. She attacked while Cúchulainn was in tutorage in Alba. Scáthach had drugged Cúchulainn to prevent his involvement in the battle but the dose was not strong enough to keep him unconscious for long. Cúchulainn joined the fight, killing Aife's son and defeating her.

A note to the end of the Táin: the men of Ulster arose from the Curse of Macha and the battle proper began with huge loss of life. Meanwhile, Mebd successfully stole the brown bull while everyone was looking elsewhere. Donn Cuailnge, the brown bull, and Finnbennach, the white bull, then fought it out until the brown bull killed and tore apart the white bull. Donn Cuailnge charged around Ireland, leaving bits of the dead Finnbenach here and there until his heart burst and he died!

Index of Authors

Sources, References & Further Reading:

1916 Poets, The *Allen Figgis, Dublin 1980*

An Duanaire: Poems of the Dispossessed 1600–1900 *(Ed. Seán Ó'Tuama trans. Thomas Kinsella) Dublin 1981*

Book of Kells, The *(Selection Peter Brown) Thames and Hudson, London 1980*

Faber Book of Contemporary Irish Poetry, The *(Ed. Paul Muldoon) Faber and Faber Ltd., London 1986*

Faber Book of Irish Verse, The *(Ed. John Montague) Faber and Faber Ltd., London 1974*

Irish Reciter, The *(Ed. Niall Toibin) The Blackstaff Press Ltd., Belfast 1986*

New Oxford Book of Irish Verse, The *(Ed. Thomas Kinsella) Oxford University Press, Oxford 1986*

Penguin Book of Irish Verse, The *(Ed. Brian Kennelly) Penguin Books, London 1970*

Allen, J. Romilly Celtic Art in Pagan and Christian Times *Methuen and Co. 1904 (reprinted Studio Editions Ltd 1993)*

Allingham, William Laurence Bloomfield in Ireland *London, 1864*

Backhouse, Janet The Lindisfarne Gospels *Phaidon Press, London 1981*

Bain, George Celtic Art The Methods of Construction *Constable, London 1951*

Brooke, Stopford A & Rollestone, T.W. A Treasury of Irish Poetry *London 1903*

Colum, Padraic The Poet's Circuits *Dolmen Press, 1981*

Davis, Courtney The Celtic Art Source Book *Blandford Press, London 1988*

Davis, Thomas National Ballads, Songs and Poems *Dublin, London 1876*

Dixon Kennedy, Mike Celtic Myth and Legend *Blandford Press, London 1996*

Farren, Robert The First Exile *Sheed & Ward Ltd., London 1944*

Ferguson, Sir Samuel Lays of the Western Geal and other Poems *London/Dublin 1897*

Ferguson, Sir Samuel The Poems of Samuel Ferguson *Allen Figgis, Dublin 1963*

Goldsmith, Oliver Selection *(Ed. Robert L Mack) Everyman/J.M. Dent 1997*

Heaney, Seamus Door into the Dark *Faber and Faber Ltd., London 1969*

Heaney, Seamus New Selected Poems 1966–1987 *Faber and Faber Ltd., London 1990*

Heaney, Seamus Seeing Things *Faber and Faber Ltd., London 1991*

Kavanagh, Patrick Selected Poems *(Ed. Antoinette Quinn) Penguin Books, London 1996*

Kinsella, Thomas The Táin *Oxford University Press, Oxford 1970*

Ledwidge, Francis The Collected Poems *London, 1919*

MacNeice, Louis The Collected Poems of Louis MacNeice *Faber & Faber Ltd., London 1966*

Mangen, J.C. Selected Poems of James Clarence Mangan *Gallery Press 1973*

Mangen, J.C. Poems, Centenary Edition *(Ed. D.J. O'Donahue), Dublin/London 1903*

Matthews, Caitlín and John The Encyclopedia of Celtic Wisdom *Element, Shaftesbury 1994*

Megaw, Ruth and Vincent Celtic Art *Thames and Hudson, London 1989*

Rolleston, T.W. Celtic Myths & Legends *Studio Editions Ltd., London 1994*

Swift, Jonathan Selected Poems *(Ed. Pat Rogers) Penguin Books, London 1993*

Synge, J.M. Plays Poems and Prose *London, 1941*

Wilde, Oscar The Works of Oscar Wilde *Wordsworth Editions Ltd, Ware, Herts. 1994*

Yeats, W.B. Selected Poetry *(Ed.Timothy Webb) Penguin Books, London 1991*